THE PITJANTJATJARA AND THEIR CRAFTS

BY PETER BROKENSHA

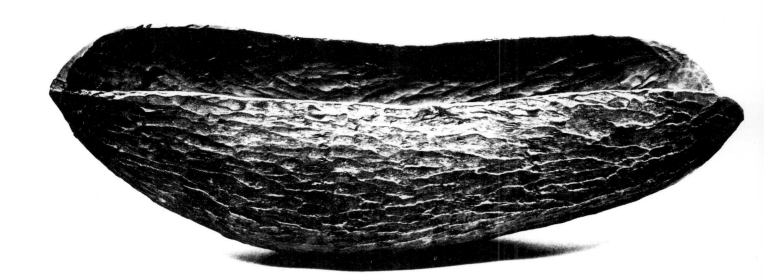

One of the major themes of this book when written in 1975 was that the return of the Pitjantjatjara people to their homelands offered them the potential to control their own lands and to determine their own future. In the foreword to the second printing in 1978 I noted the progress which the people had made towards achieving land rights from the South Australian Government and how they had formed their own political organisation the Pitjantjatjara Council. It is appropriate for the reader to ask what has happened to the Pitjantjatjara since 1978 with respect to the vital issues of land rights, self-determination, health, the return to the homelands movement and the integrity of their culture and their crafts. It is impossible to do more than lightly brush the surface of some of these complex issues in a short foreword.

LAND RIGHTS

The most important event was the achievement of land rights that occurred when the Pitjantjatjara Land Rights Act became law on march 18th 1981. This Act vested 103,000 square kilometres of land under inalienable freehold title in an unique incorporation of all Pitjantjatjara people — the Anangu Pitjantjatjaraku. The other important provisions of the Act as described by Toyne and Vachon (1984:108) were:

*All non Pitjantjatjara (with some statutory exceptions such as police and members of parliament) would require permits from the land holding incorporation to enter the lands. Miners wishing to enter and explore must first be approved by the Department of Mines and Energy and then negotiate directly with the land holding incorporation. Any agreement reached would include social and environmental protection provisions and the right of the **anangu** to receive payments of compensation for disturbance to their lands, the people and their way of life. Any mineral or petroleum explorer aggrieved by a refusal of the incorporation to allow entry could apply for arbitration before a Supreme Court judge. In considering his decision the arbitrator was heavily directed towardss protecting Aboriginal interests. The judge had to consider the importance of the exploration to the state and the nation.*

The land holding incorporation is also entitled to one third of the Crown royalties on minerals and petroleum extracted on the lands. Another third is distributed to other Aboriginal people in the state and the government receives the final third.

Hailed as model land rights legislation it was not won without a long frustating struggle. As predicted in the 1978 foreword to the second printing of this book the [then] Premier of South Australia, Don Dunstan, did place a Bill before Parliament in November 1978 to provide land rights for the Pitjantjatjara. The first set back for the Pitjantjatjara occurred when Dunstan resigned due to ill health in February 1979 before the Bill was passed. The Labor Government then lost office in September 1979 to the Tonkin Liberal Government. In February 1980 the Pitjantjatjara travelled to Adelaide, camped on the Victoria Park Racecourse in the heart of the city and forceably put their case to the new government and the media. The story of how this uncommited and somewhat uncomprehending government was finally convinced to pass very similar land rights legislation has been well told by Toyne and Vachon (1984) and by Hope (in print). The favourable outcome is a tribute to the unswerving determination of the Pitjantjatjara people to have title to their rightful lands and in no small part due to the brilliance and tenacity of the Pitjantjatjara advisers and lawyers, particularly Philip Toyne. This Act applies only to Pitjantjatjara lands within South Australia. The Pitjantjatjara and their neighbours the Nyaangantjara in Western Australia have only in late 1986 been offered a leasehold over their traditional lands. The Pitjantjatjara and their eastern neighbours the Yakuntjatjara who are the traditional owners of the Ayers Rock area in the Northern Territory received title to their lands in 1985 with a 99-year lease back to the Australian National Parks and Wildlife Service.

HEALTH

The moves towards Aboriginal control of health services have continued. In 1982 a state-wide community controlled South Austrlian Aboriginal Trachoma and Eye Health Committee was formed to co-ordinate Ophthalmologist screening and treatment programs throughout Aboriginal communities in South Australia (Foley, 1984:22).

In the Pitjantjatjara lands a further important step was the formation of the Pitjantjatjara Community controlled Nganampa Health Council Inc. in 1984. This Council provides primary preventative and public health services as well as education and community developmentk services throughout the Pitjantjatjara lands. The Council operates seven community health centres, has a total medical and paramedical staff of forty and attends to some 45,000 patients per year.

In 1985 the Mutitjulu/Imanpa Health Service was also established at Ayers Rock.

Plate A   Amata Settlement 1984

Despite all the work being done, the inputs from European society of diseases, processed foods and alcohol have continued to maintain Aboriginal health standards at an appallingly low level compared with levels in the white population. One of the major health/social problems which the Pitjantjatjara (and other groups) face is the incidence of regular petrol sniffing amongst children and young adults.

> *In some communities well over 50% of children from ages 5 and 6 years to 20 years are regular daily petrol sniffers.*
> *(Foley, 1984:50)*

> *At Amata in May 1986 there were some 50-60 sniffers in a school age population of between 80 and 90.*
> *(Hope, 1986:19)*

As the white community has learnt more of this problem through visits to settlements by the media and politicians so concern has grown to find solutions. Many have been tried over many years with apparent success in some communities and little or none in others. Some informed researchers suggest that petrol sniffing is one obvious and distressing symbol of the effect of white culture contact.

THE HOMELAND MOVEMENT

Since 1978 the Pitjantjatjara homeland answer movement has continued to grow as more and more Pitjantjatjara disperse themselves over their traditional lands. I am indebted to Ushma Scales who has worked and lived with the Pitjantjatjara since the mid-1970s for the following up-to-date information. Mr. Scales has categorised the geographic settlement pattern of the Pitjantjatjara in the following way.

1. Large Settlements

All the original settlements and missions set up by the governments or churches have remained, although in most cases the population is smaller. Many of the settlements have taken on a softer Aboriginal ambience as under Pitjantjatjara control the old colonial style emphasis on order and neatness has faded as trees and vegetation have been let to grow where they may (See Plate A). These large settlements tend to contain a diverse and sometimes artificial collection of Pitjantjatjara at a place which may not be their traditional country but offers other attractions such as schools and stores. It is interesting to note that Pipalyatjara which is described in Chapter 5 as a small typical homeland camp when I lived there in 1975 is now categorised by Scales as a major settlement with between 100 and 200 people, resident whites and a store and school etc.

2. Homelands

These are locations to which the traditional 'owners' of an area and their families have returned. These may be permanent camps or places where the members of the appropriate descent groups live occasionally.

3. Outstations

These are camps which have no particular sacred significance and no identifiable local descent group in residence. There are usually outstations relatively close to a major settlement.

4. Ceremonial Homelands

These are particularly significant sacred sites where large numbers of Pitjantjatjara gather periodically to perform ceremonies specifically related to that site but there is no permanent habitation.

5. Occasional Homelands

These are camps where the descent group owners do not live permanently but visit from major settlements at weekends or when vehicles are available to take them there.

In 1975 there was only a handful of homelands on the Pitjantjatjara lands. The growth of the decentralisation movement has been such that in 1986 Scales recorded in South Australia alone the following numbers of locations of the types mentioned:

17	Permanent Homelands
27	Occasional Homelands
3	Ceremonial Homelands
19	Permanent Outstations
4	Occasional Outstations
70	Total

If the adjacent lands of the Pitjantjatjara and their neighbours in Western Australia and the Northern Territory are included the number of homelands and outstations swells to 116. Some of these are shown on Plate B.

Scales also points out some of the factors which are inhibiting the development of the homeland movement in the central desert area:

There is a problem in knowing which government agency is responsible for what because multiple agencies are involved reporting to three state governments and the federal government.

Each of the four governments involved has different ideas about appropriate models and directions for the homeland movement.

Educational support for homelands has been inadequate and there is litle recreational activity for youth. These factors have skewed the population in the homelands towards the elderly.

Because many homelands are very isolated and in a harsh environment their ability to survive is dependent on the supply link for food and maintaining water bores. This link is often fragile and dependent on the homeland group having a reliable vehicle.

However despit these problems the homeland movement has continued to develop and grow.

CULTURAL INTEGRITY

The pervasiveness and appeal of European artifacts and technology would seem to provide overwhelming threats to Aboriginal culture. However, the Pitjantjatjara have demonstrated a determination to maintain their cultural identity and are learning to adapt European organisation and technology for that purpose. The way the Pitjantjatjara Council has developed and how it is used by all the Pitjantjatjara as their political and administrative organ demonstrates this. Communications over this vast landscape are improving. In 1984 a major road building program began and most homelands have solar powered radio transmitter/receivers to enable the people to receive the Pitjantjatjara Council news broadcasts or to communicate with other centres on their 'Chatter Channel'. An historic event in 1986 was the granting by the Australian Government of the only central Australian television transmitting licence to the Aboriginal people through the Central Australian Aboriginal Media Association. By this enlightened decision, made against considerable other commercial interest pressure, the Australian Government has hopefully ameliorated for a time at least the threat to their culture from the effects of foreign junk television. Hope (1986:35) suggests that the use of video and television may provide some contructive and elegant alternatives to enable the Pitjantjatjara to revivify their relationships with the land in the face of a sedentary life style.

PITJANTJATJARA CRAFTS

The Pitjantjatjara people are now making more of their beautiful high quality traditional and adapted crafts than ever before. In 1984 the people established their own regional craft co-operative. Maruku Arts and Crafts, to handle the development and marketing of craft from the whole Western Desert region. The co-operative is based at Ayers Rock where it has a major retail outlet. Every month the buyers from Maruku travel up to 1,000 kilometres to all the settlements and homeland to buy the craft produced by over 400 Pitjantjatjara craftsmen and craftswomen.

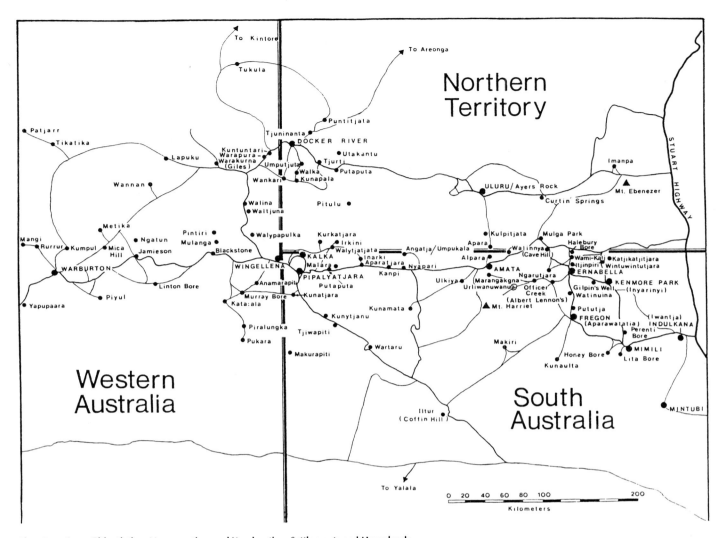

Plate B   Some Pitjantjatjara Nyaangantjara and Yangkuntjara Settlements and Homelands.
(Reproduced by permission from Report of the South Australian Aboriginal Customary Law Committee — Adelaide 1984).

THE FUTURE

As this brief foreword indicates, a lot has happened to the Pitjantjatjara since 1978. As for the future I refer again to Toyne and Vachon (1984:156) who were so closely involved in events over this period.

Anangu are no longer the same people whom Duguid met in the 1930s. Nor are they the same people who first met and spoke to Dunstan about their land and land rights. And they are not the 'traditional' backwash of Australian society presented so often in the media. Along with their unique religious and social system, they are developing new organisations and relationships to solve the problems of a new world and, in some measure, to exert control over their development.

When and how the Pitjantjatjara will finally be able to fully control and determine their future remains as always largely in the hands of the white society who have been slow to listen, to learn and to understand the values and needs of a civilisation which has outlasted their own by millenia.

Peter Brokensha
Adelaide, February 1987

REFERENCES

Foley, G.E.   1984. "Report of the Committee of Review into Aboriginal Health in South Australia". S.A. Government Adelaide.

Hope, D.A.C.   1986. "Reshaping the Dream — A Transcultural Analysis of Contemporary Problems in Pitjantjatjara Society". Paper submitted to the 12th Congress of the International Academy of Comparative Law, Sydney, August 1984.

Hope D.A.C.   1987. "The Menticulturists" — In Print.

Toyne Phillip and   1984. "Growing up the Country — The
Vachon Daniel   Pitjantjatjara Struggle for their Land" McPhee Gribble/Penguin Books Melbourne.

FOREWORD TO SECOND PRINTING

It is only three years since the publication of this book. It is indicative of the rapid rate of change in Aboriginal societies that a great deal has happened to the Pitjantjatjara in such a short period.

The most significant development has been the formation by the Pitjantjatjara, Yakuntjatjara and Ngatatjara people of a political organisation, the Pitjantjatjara Council, embracing Aboriginals living in the huge triangle bounded by Warburton (W.A.), Docker River (N.T.) and Indulkana (S.A.).
The reasons for its formation in October, 1976, have been clearly expressed by the Council's secretary:—

> *"The Pitjantjatjara Council was made to help people understand and see how the Pitjantjatjara people work and what the Pitjantjatjara people want. Also the Pitjantjatjara Council was made so that white people can see and understand us more and also to see that we have one law and we are one, no matter where we come from, we have this one law and we've got one law all the time. We still have this law and that's why we are asking for land because this land is ours. It belongs to us. We kept this land for a long, long time and that's why we want you to see very clearly that this land is ours. We don't want to have two laws — white man's law and Aboriginal law. We want you to see that this land is the Pitjantjatjaras' land. That's why the Pitjantjatjara Council was made. So that we can fight and get our land back, because this land is very important to us and we have strong rules and strong laws."*

Until very recently the Pitjantjatjara had never doubted their ownership of their land. However, once doubts were raised by news of the Northern Territory Land Rights Legislation they acted quickly to organise their Council and politely yet firmly ask the South Australian Government to protect their ownership of their land. They received a most sympathetic hearing from the Premier of South Australia, Mr Don Dunstan, who has long supported and progressively legislated for Aboriginal rights. As a result a Government Working Party was set up to ascertain the wishes of the Pitjantjatjara with regard to ownership and management of their land and legislation is now scheduled for 1978, which will vest freehold title in the Pitjantjatjara people of some 90,000 square kilometres of land comprising the present North West Aboriginal Reserve and the adjacent pastoral properties of Ernabella, Kenmore Park and Mimili.

Another major achievement has been in the field of health care. In 1975 I wrote: *"Nobody really cares about doing anything positive to alleviate short or long term problems of Aboriginal health in this area."* Happily, this is no long true. In 1976 the National Trachoma and Eye Health Program organised by the Royal Australian College of Opthalmologists and funded the Australian Government commenced working in the Pitjantjatjara area. They found an alarming incidence of eye disease with, for example, a trachoma rate in children under 11 years of age varying from 33% at Ernabella to 80% at Wingelina. Treatment programs and where necessary, surgery were carried out and follow up programs are still continuing with the result that sight impairment and blindness have been markedly reduced. Many tragic examples of neglect were rectified by the work of the trachoma team's surgeons, such as an old Pitjantjatjara man from Pipalyatjara, who could see again after being completely blind for fifteen years. The most significant development in the field of health was the commencement early in 1978 of the Pitjantjatjara Homelands Health Service. This has come about largely because of the determined efforts of Mr Glendle Schrader, who was community adviser at Pipalyatjara from 1975 to 1977. Apalled at the lack of provision for health care or training by the responsible State health authorities, he sought and gained approval from the Federal Minister for Aboriginal Affairs, Mr Ian Viner, for funding to initiate a health program to cover all Pitjantjatjara homeland centres. The service in now providing health care to at least 15 homeland communities dispersed over an area of approximately 100,000 square kilometres in Western Australia, Northern Territory and South Australia. The service is unique and that it is controlled by the Aboriginal people themselves through the Pitjantjatjara Council. Other than a minimal European staff of doctor, administrator and health worker educator, it has all Aboriginal staff including seventeen Pitjantjatjara health workers providing grass roots services in their own communities.

The decentralisation initiative of the Pitjantjatjara has accelerated since 1975 with new homeland centres, as they are now referred to, established at Kunamatta, Kunytjanu, Iltor in South Australia, Walytjitjata in the Northern Territory and Kata:la in Western Australia to name only a few. These homeland centres have no permanent white presence and are serviced with stores somewhat irregularly from Amata.

Despite the positive changes I have reported, the Pitjantjatjara are at some locations facing increasing problems arising from the withdrawal of the European authority structure in the name of fostering self determination. Because there has been little emphasis on training and development of Pitjantjatjara, particularly in spheres of organisation and management, the resulting authority and leadership vacuum is causing a major breakdown in services and control at some locations.

At this critical period in their history, the Pitjantjatjara don't need European buildings and facilities but do need trained, energetic and sympathetic people who will work as clients of the people, maintaining services and training the Pitjantjatjara in the management of their own affairs. These Europeans must not only develop management skills in the Pitjantjatjara, but also believe in the future of self reliance for the people.

Peter Brokensha
September 1978

CONTENTS

INTRODUCTION

All over the northern and central parts of Australia Aboriginal people who for a generation or more have been institutionalised on missions and settlements are leaving them to set up their own small decentralised communities back on their traditional lands. Whilst some groups have tried this spasmodically for many years it is now being undertaken within a new Government framework which avows a policy of self determination for Aboriginal people.

This monograph deals with one such group of Pitjantjatjara who left Amata settlement and Ernabella mission to establish new self determining settlements in the Mann and Tomkinson Ranges in the far north-west of South Australia.

The history of the peoples contact with Europeans is discussed, their departure from their homeland and their return. The way of life of the Pitjantjatjara in a new decentralised community is also outlined and the range as well as the method of manufacture of traditional and adapted crafts is described. The development of the artifact industry is traced and its importance to the people discussed.

The final chapter discusses some of the problems the people are facing in this new situation and suggests ways in which these groups may be assisted to survive.

This work is based on intermittent contact with Amata settlement since 1971 and a period of approximately three months spent with the Pitjantjatjara at Amata and a decentralised settlement early in 1975.

Because of the relative brevity of contact this paper is presented as a set of preliminary observations. It is written now as it is felt that in the interests of the groups themselves, it is important in a rapidly changing situation for people involved in Aboriginal affairs to have ready access to all available information. Some of the strongest impressions gained were:

- This decentralisation initiative is not only a reaction to a situation imposed on them by Europeans but is motivated by their traditional religious relationship with the land to which they have returned.

- The problem of adapting traditional norms of conduct to new situations is creating stresses in these communities particularly in the areas of political organisation and leadership.

- Maintenance of a strong traditional craft activity is important to the people both culturally and economically and should be given every assistance and encouragement.

- The people themselves are determined to make a success of their own self determining decentralised communities. However, there are signs that this desire could be frustrated unless Government administrators are prepared to give the type of patient and unobtrusive help for which the people are asking without being subject to excessive pressures towards assimilation and modernisation.

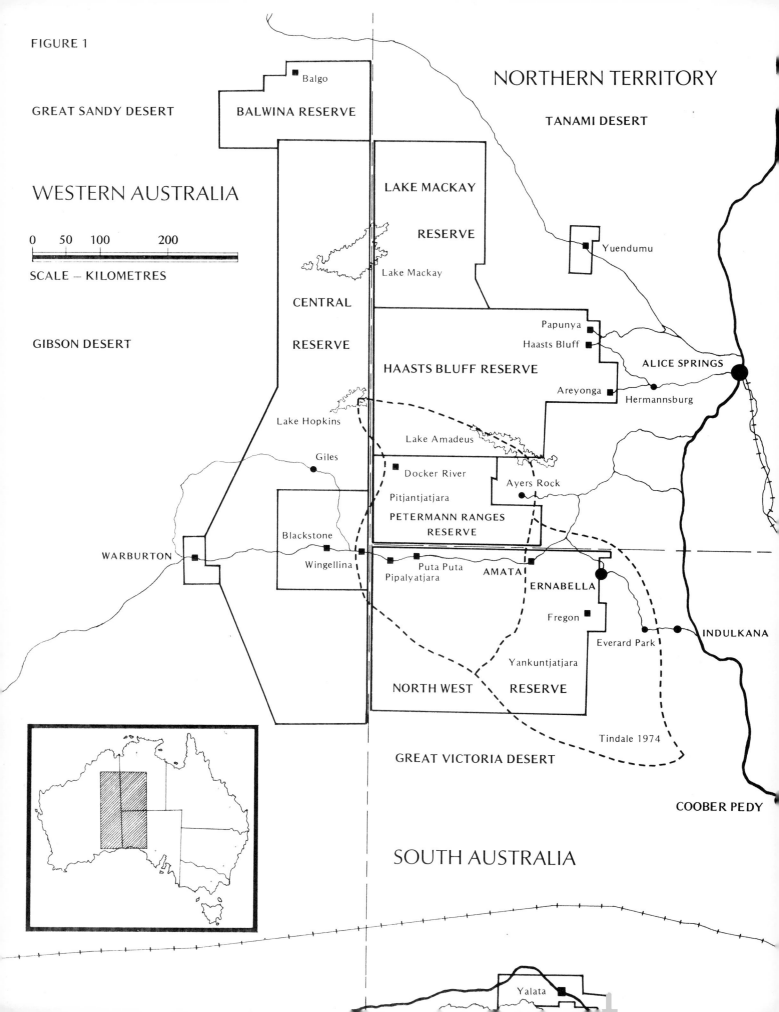

FIGURE 1

1 THE PITJANTJATJARA AND THEIR LAND

The people whom we now refer to as Pitjantjatjara presently live and probably lived for a very long time in an area generally referred to as the Western Desert. Berndt (1959:81) describes the Western Desert as the region which extends across western South Australia into eastern and north-eastern Western Australia and includes part of the mountainous range country of northern South Australia and central Australia. The area therefore includes part of the Gibson and Great Victoria deserts as well as the Petermann, Rawlinson, Warburton, Blackstone, Tomkinson, Mann and Musgrave Ranges. (see figure 1).

Whilst the area does not fit the popular conception of a sandy wasteland it quite correctly falls into the geographical classification of a desert. Evaporation exceeds precipitation, there are no permanent streams and rainfall is low but extremely variable from year to year.

The average annual rainfall over most of the Western Desert area is of the order of 200 mm but this is quite misleading because of the extreme variations. Figure 2 shows the annual rainfall at Ernabella in the Musgrave Ranges from 1936-1974 which demonstrates a variability from approximately 50 mm to 750 mm annually.

The annual average evaporation is in excess of 3000 mm per annum and the sky is generally monotonously cloudless with a daily average of 9.6 hours of bright sunshine at Giles weather station near the Rawlinson Ranges. Daytime temperatures are consistently very hot in summer and temperate in winter. The January and July mean of maximum recorded daily temperatures at Giles are 30°C and 19°C respectively. Nights are temperate in summer and cold in winter. The January and July mean of minimum daily temperatures at Giles are 24°C and 7°C respectively. Occasional shade temperatures range from over 46°C in summer to below freezing point in winter.

Rainfall records from the periphery of the Western Desert at Laverton W.A. (from 1900) and from Hermansburg N.T. (from 1888) confirm the pattern depicted for Ernabella of variable and uncertain rainfall with irregularly recurring periods of several summer months with virtually no rainfall at all. This coupled with the high evaporation rate would indicate uncertainty of water supply was a factor of pre-contact Aboriginal life in the Western Desert. Certainly natural rockhole catchments could not be relied upon as was evident in the Tomkinson Ranges in February 1975 when after only two months with little rain most of the major rockholes were dry. Just how long during periods of drought the people could obtain water from soaks, claypans or from

the water bearing trees, shrubs and roots listed by Johnston (1941:34-35) has yet to be fully explored as has the precise relationship between rainfall and the availability of vegetable foods and desert fauna.

Nevertheless it could be assumed that the Western Desert was a difficult environment for its inhabitants and according to Mabbut (1971:78) such climatic changes as have occurred over the last 30,000 years are unlikely to have changed this. It is probable that in this environment the Pitjantjatjara were forced to adopt a pattern of wide ranging mobility in search of food and water.

In a discussion of the Pitjantjatjara and their material culture it is relevant to consider who exactly the Pitjantjatjara are, where their traditional country was and what forms of local organisation they had. The answers to these questions are not straightforward and involve considerable conjecture. Whilst, as will be described later, the Pitjantjatjara are now widely dispersed and new lifestyles and forms or organisation are being developed. The manner in which groups of the people are returning to certain areas to set up their own settlements may yet provide some new insights to these questions.

Tindale (1940 and 1974) as part of his monumental work on the distribution of Australian tribes, defined the boundaries of the Pitjantjatjara. These are shown, along with the boundaries of the Yankuntjatjara, on figure 1. He argues that groups called tribes in the Western Desert have the same political value as tribes in other parts of Australia and that they occupied discrete areas.

Others disagree with this view. With regard to language Douglas (1964:1-3) points out there is one language across the whole of the Western Desert area with many dialects. What he calls "nicknames" are given to various dialects. The people in the eastern part of the area call the people who use the word *"pitjantja"* instead of *"yankuntja"* for "came" the Pitjantjatjara, whilst conversely the Pitjantjatjara call them the Yankuntjatjara, *(tjara* = with or having). However, as he points out there are so many other overlapping variations in the vocabulary that a major division on this basis would be unreasonable.

The people themselves seldom refer to their language or to themselves as Pitjantjatjara. However, this is changing under the influence of more contact with Europeans who use the term Pitjantjatjara to identify both the people and the language over most of the Western Desert area. It could be argued that Europeans have constructed a total identity for the Pitjantjatjara which did not exist in the past and does not exist today.

To reinforce this contention and to explain the manner in which some Western Desert groups are now redispersing, it is relevant to refer to the conclusions reached by researchers with regard to traditional forms of local organisation.

A basic factor, as Hiatt (1962:284) points out, is to distinguish two kinds of relationships between people and land, the economic relationships and the ritual relationships. Based on extensive field work with Western Desert people at Ooldea in 1941 and in eastern Western Australia in 1957-9, Berndt (1959:95-106) identified five types of social units.

The first was the dialectical unit of groups speaking the same dialect. As Berndt pointed out this was an "open" group territorially anchored only in relation to the local groups that comprised it. Whilst minor differences in dialect are still readily recognisable as one moves from Ernabella west these dialectical distinctions are becoming blurred particularly as the Pitjantjatjara literacy programs in schools are largely based on the dictionary and grammar prepared at Ernabella.

Then there were three types of social units based in Hiatt's terms on ritual relationships between the people and the land

■ Local patrilineal descent groups whose members had special spiritual and ritual ties with certain totemic sites. These groups could be termed the land owning groups.

■ Religious cult groups consisting of adult male members of local groups whose totemic sites lie along adjoining sections of one ancestral route.

■ Wide ritual groups of up to 200-300 people who would come together seasonally for major ceremonies.

The fifth type of group is what Berndt called the horde whose members had an economic relationship with the land over which they moved in search of sustenance. This unit was the land occupying group which had as its core the male members of a local group plus unmarried females plus wives and children of male members but could include transients and members of other patrilineal descent groups.

Berndt concludes that the term tribe as generally used is not applicable to any social unit found in the Western Desert and as Hiatt (1962:285) points out there is considerable evidence to suggest that the totemic sites of many patrilineal descent groups were not enclosed by territorial boundaries and that the food seeking or land occupying groups moved freely over the totemic site areas of other groups. Thus it seems that in the total Western Desert area where the people had a demonstrably similar culture and language, there were no meaningful discrete groups either socially or territorially which is important if attempts are made to define traditional territorial boundaries in relation to land rights.

Whilst more work has to be done on the subject it is relevant to record some preliminary observations on the visibility and importance of the traditional groupings in present day Pitjantjatjara society.

Dealing with each of the five groupings in turn, the first dialectical group appears to have become blurred and largely lost significance. However, the descent groups whose members have special ritual ties with certain totemic sites still form a strong cohesive unit and it is this grouping that appears to have determined the pattern of the decentralisation initiative. The people who have ritual ties with the *malu* (kangaroo) totemic sites have moved to Pipalyatjara near where their sites are located, whilst the *ili* (fig) totem people are organising to return to Kunamatta near their sites and likewise the *ngintaka* (goana) people are organising to return to Lake Wilson and so on. The membership of these groups is no longer as clearly defined as it may have been traditionally because not all constellations of sites have a bore in the proximity, which is an essential requirement for a new camp under present conditions. For example there are men at Pipalyatjara with ties to the *nyinyi* (finch) totem sites in the Bellrock Ranges who have expressed a strong desire to return and live there but meanwhile have moved to the closest available camp.

Feelings occasionally run high between these groups, with each group denigrating the importance of the others sites at least in the presence of Europeans. My impression is that this is to some extent a new rivalry engendered by competition between groups for European resources. However, it is evident that members of these totemic groups or a slightly wider group embracing people with affiliations to sites in adjoining geographical areas, perceive and articulate a notion of separate group identity. This wider grouping may relate in some way to Berndt's second grouping arising from affiliations with adjoining sections of one ancestral route although this is by no means clear and the question of how this new political factor of competition for European resources is affecting local group composition is yet to be explored fully. Yengoyan (1970: 83-85) touched on this subject when discussing the relationship men claimed with the Mount Davies (Pipalyatjara) area in order to gain access to the intermittent chrysoprase mining activity there in 1966. He noted how in one case which is relevant to the grouping under discussion, a man gained access to the group because of his ritual relationship with the adjacent *tjurki* (owl) totemic sites.

Despite these developments Berndt's third wider ritual groups are still very much in evidence. The availability of vehicles has enabled this activity to be widened and increased far more than would have been possible traditionally. During the period from June 1974 to June 1975 a group of about 200 Pitjantjatjara travelled to Papunya, to all the sites between Amata and Blackstone and to Yalata.
The final economic unit, the horde, has little significance today although vehicles are used to range widely in search of game and it is interesting to note that there is still no overt sense of territorial ownership of resources. Any Aboriginals may go anywhere and hunt without the local group feeling that their land is being wrongly utilised.

The above is intended to give a general idea of the Pitjantjatjara and their land. The remaining sections of this monograph will be mainly concerned with the history and present way of life of one specific group who have moved back to the vicinity of their totemic sites in the Tomkinson Ranges.

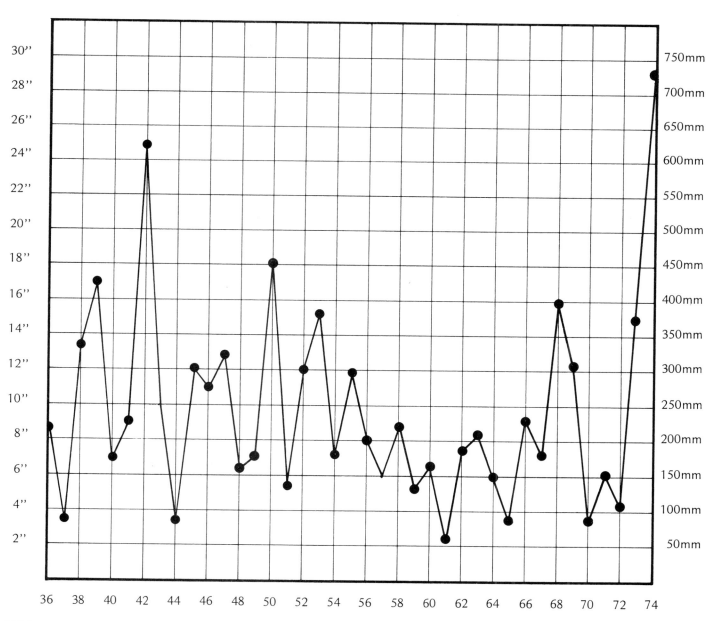

2   THE CONTACT PERIOD

European contact with the Western Pitjantjatjara had until the 1930's been negligible and even today intrusion by Europeans into their traditional lands in the Mann and Tomkinson Ranges is very minimal. The area was not visited at all until the expeditions of Giles in 1872 and 1873-4, Gosse in 1873 and Forrest in 1874. It was first surveyed by Carruthers (1892) in 1888-1890 followed by the Elder Scientific Expedition which traversed the southern and western part of the area in 1891. Helms (1896:237-332) recorded information about the customs and material culture of the people as did Basedow (1904:12-51) who was a member of the first Government prospecting expedition into the Mann and Tomkinson Ranges in 1903.

Occasional small prospecting parties visited the area at the turn of the century and up until the 1930's. These prospectors evidently had little contact with the Aboriginal people and generally were disinterested in and fearful of the people whose lands they were traversing. Terry, who led a prospecting expedition through the area in 1930 using camels and the first truck, records (Terry 1932:110) that although the Tomkinson Range people were quite friendly he made it clear that he did not want them within 200 yards of his camp and "we wished them gone for ever and a day".

However, unwittingly these prospectors performed a valuable service for the Western Desert people. Their prospecting expeditions found nothing of value and they exploded the myth that the area was rich in gold. As the country was too rugged and the rainfall too sparse and unreliable to attract potential pastoralists and as there appeared to be no mineral wealth, ideas of economic exploitation were forgotten and apart from occasional doggers seeking the dingo scalp bounty, the area west of the Musgraves was left undisturbed until the 1930's. During this period the policy of Governments was to isolate and "protect" the remaining tribal members of a race for whom little hope of survival was held. Aboriginal reserves were created in the area; in Western Australia (The Central Reserve 1918), in the Northern Territory (The South West Reserve 1920) and in South Australia (The North West Reserve 1921). These three adjoining reserves now comprise an area of approximately 100,000 square miles (see figure 1). The gazetting of reserves provided no real territorial security for the Western Desert people against political or economic exploitation as shown by the intrusions into the area in connection with the Woomera Rocket Range in the 1950's, the excision of 7,000 square miles in the Wingellina area in 1958 for nickel mining operations and the excision of the area containing Ayers Rock and the Olgas in the same year.

Nevertheless, a combination of the fortuitous circumstances of isolated location, climate, lack of minerals or pastoral potential and the creation of reserves, meant that intensive European contact with all its consequences for an Aboriginal society did not occur until very recently. The first more detailed record of the way of life of the Western Desert people was made by Tindale who visited the area from the Musgraves to the Mann Ranges in 1933. He recorded details of myths and ceremonies and made valuable films of the people who were "still wandering freely as hunting nomads in their own country . . . subject to few outside influences . . . they had not yet obtained any metal substitutes for their stone tools" (Tindale 1935:221). From Tindale's records and films and from the accounts of the older Pitjantjatjara men it is clear that at that time the Western Desert people were living a truly traditional nomadic life.

The older Tomkinson Range men remember well the period before they saw white men. They were able to show me the rockholes where they were born and the constellation of rockholes and sacred sites which were the focus of their true country. As will be discussed later their material culture was meagre — for the women wooden bowls, a digging stick and a pair of grinding stones (see plate 2:1). The men hunted with a spear thrower and spears and possessed little else. From the reports and films, mainly by Tindale, it appears that this traditional lifestyle continued right up into the late 1930's and even later. The first sign of European influence was the use of pieces of sharpened discarded metal in place of stone tools. Plate 2:2, from a photograph taken by Dr. Hackett, in 1933 shows the addition of a steel tipped adzing tool to the basic spear thrower and spear kit.

Plate 2:1 The Pitjantjatjara in common with other Aboriginal groups were nomadic hunter/gatherers who continually moved about their tribal lands in a never-ending quest for food. Pitjantjatjara women moving camp in the Musgrave Ranges in 1933.

Plate 2:2 The Pitjantjatjara had few tools and weapons. This man carried only a spearthrower, two spears and an adzing tool. Musgrave Ranges, 1933.

3 THE DEPARTURE

Well before the 1930's Western Desert people had been moving south to Ooldea Water and along the transcontinental railway as reported by Daisy Bates (1921:73-78). Detailed studies by Berndt (1941:1-20) and Johnston (1941:33-65) indicate not only some permanent migration southwards to European settlements but a whole complex pattern of tribal routes which were used before contact for trade and ceremonial purposes.

In this account I am concerned more narrowly with the Western Desert people who were living in areas around the Mann and Tomkinson Ranges and their departure from this area. Whilst a few of the people both to the east and west of this area had moved to live in towns and cattle stations, the major impetus to movement was provided by the establishment of missions in the Western Desert area itself in the 1930's.

The first mission in the western edge of the area was established at Warburton in 1934. Tindale visited Warburton mission in 1935 and his comments (Tindale 1936:483) are very relevant. "This depot under the auspices of the United Aborigines Mission trades with the natives, receiving dingo scalps valued at £1 each in Western Australia in return for European white flour and second hand clothing transported to the Warburton Range at high cost (£40 per ton). It is to be hoped that the presence of a nucleus of European occupation so far (330 miles) beyond the white man's country is justified and will outweigh the undoubted disadvantage of having the natives (who are at present free from serious epidemic diseases) in close proximity to Europeans with the probabi-

lity of transmitting to them the simple ailments of our race — coughs, colds, influence and measles — whose ravages elsewhere have been stated to be a serious factor in depopulation". Tindale's fears were well founded as by 1956 when Grayden visited the area as leader of a W.A. Government select committee he reported (Grayden 1956:9) that 80% of the children at the mission had active trachoma and the incidence of pneumonia, other chest complaints, syphilis or yaws was high. His later book (Grayden 1957) details attempts to discredit the committee findings by officials and sections of the press.

More significantly in the eastern fringes by the 1930's European influence had started to intrude into the Everard and Musgrave Ranges with the granting of pastoral leases one of which (Ernabella) was taken over as a Presbyterian mission in 1937. Soon after Ernabella was established many of the Mann and Tomkinson Range people settled there while some were living at Mulga Park Station and finally with the establishment of Musgrave Park (later called Amata) Government settlement in 1961, the settlement of these western people, outside their traditional estate, was well established. Berndt (1941:4) suggests that even well before this the Pitjantjatjara had been moving eastwards displacing the Jankuntjatjara who with the Antakirinja, had since 1917, been moving gradually south to Ooldea. Elkin (1939:203) states that the western South Australian people had been in a continuous state of migration southwards for some decades and that this movement was in progress before the coming of the white man and explains the similarities of dialects, kinship systems and mythology over such a vast area and also the difficulty of fixing definite tribal boundaries and names. However, some researchers with more intimate knowledge of the Pitjantjatjara and the Jankuntjatjara in their own lands, have suggested that any concept of permanent migration is alien to the Western Desert people whose whole existence involved movement and admixture of dialectical groups for social and ceremonial reasons but still with some form of anchorage and return to their own core constellation of totemic sites.

To the north also the Pitjantjatjara people from the Petermann Ranges had according to Long (1963:4) been moving east to cattle stations, Hermannsburg mission, Alice Springs and Jay Creek settlement. Strehlow (1968:9) comments "on my own camel journeys in 1936 and 1939 I met only a few scattered groups of nomads in the very heart of the Pitjantjatjara country the Petermann Ranges." The establishment of ration depots at Haasts Bluff (1940) and at Areyonga (1943) attracted more Petermann Range people and both these places became Government settlements in 1953. When Munn (1965:1) was at Areyonga almost all the people, at times over 300, called themselves Pitjantjatjara and identified their homeland mainly as individual rockholes and sites in the Petermann Ranges.

Thus progressively the Western Desert people had left their own country. This movement which started in earnest in the late 1930's and 1940's was forcibly finalised in the 1950's when Government patrols were sent to ensure that no people were still anywhere in the vicinity of Woomera Rocket Range which virtually traversed the whole area.

Given that the people had strong religious ties with their own country why then over this period did they leave to live in missions and settlements mostly well outside their traditional estate? The reason was generally given by the people themselves, and has been accepted, as simply that they wanted the white man's goods such as tea, flour and sugar. With reference to the Walbiri to the north Meggitt (1965:23,27) points out that they were content to maintain a pattern of sporadic contact with Europeans indefinitely as it enabled them to obtain some of the goods they desired yet keep returning to their homeland to maintain their independence. He further suggests that after the extremely severe drought of 1924-1929 which had forced the people out of the desert, they became so accustomed to the new white man's goods and other material possessions that they had no desire to return to the rigorous life in the bush.

Whilst more research is needed on this subject I feel the reasons why the Pitjantjatjara left their homeland and have stayed away from it for up to 20 or 30 years, are more complex than suggested by Meggitt for the Walbiri.

The older men now back in the Tomkinsons, left there in the late 1930's early 1940's and mostly went to Ernabella. They say that there was plenty of water and plenty of game around then but white men came out and said there was a good camp at Ernabella so they went. This in itself was not a major step as traditionally the people had travelled into the Musgraves for ceremonies or when food or water were short. However, the reasons why they stayed at Ernabella and later at Amata are not as clear. The people certainly in these earlier years gained nothing in material possessions, nor in living conditions, as their camps on the fringes of the mission and settlement were composed of humpies and *wiltjas* and they suffered from new sicknesses and many more of their infants died. They could rarely hunt or eat kangaroo and emu meat which they prized but flour and particularly sugar were available

in greater quantities and without the effort of collecting and grinding edible grass seeds or collecting honey ants which were the traditional equivalent. This new source of food, even if it was strange and often inadequate, was available with a minimum of effort and irrespective of the season. It is most likely that this was the major reason why the people came to and at least initially stayed at Missions and settlements. But they did not lose their desire to return to their own country and to renew their spiritual links with it. This hypothesis is supported by the immediate return to their homeland of many of the people as soon as it was known that the authorities were no longer opposed to decentralised settlements.

So at varying times during the period of about 1930-1950 all the local groups comprising Western Desert people left their own country and became dispersed over a wide area. They went to and are mostly still living at Amata Settlement, Pukatja (formerly Ernabella mission), Aparwatatja (formerly Fregon outstation), Areyonga, Indulkana, Warburton Settlements with smaller numbers at cattle station/stores like Curtin Springs and Mt. Ebenezer or at towns like Alice Springs, Oodnadatta and Laverton.

The treatment the Western Desert people received in these new situations varied. Occasionally the owners of cattle stations were kindly, sympathetic men (The Pitjantjatjara men who went to Mulga Park Station in the 1940's still speak of the help and friendship they received) but more often than not they were subjected to brutality, prejudice and rank exploitation (see Stevens 1974).

At missions also the attitudes of the missionaries and their treatment of the people varied greatly. At Ernabella the policy of the founder Dr. Duguid (1972:115) was "There was to be no compulsion nor imposition of our way of life on the Aborigines, nor deliberate interference with tribal custom". At the other end of the scale at Jigalong, the missionaries main aim was to "save the souls" of the Aboriginals, whom they considered "children of the devil" and "lost in darkness". All school age children were placed in dormitories to remove them from what the missionaries considered to be the "pernicious influence of camp life". (Tonkinson 1974:33).

On Government settlements the people tended to become statistics in the fluctuating and unwieldy processes of Government and bureaucracy. (See Biskup 1973 with reference to Western Australia). The attitudes of settlement staff towards Aboriginals also varied from extremes of high regard for the people to disregard and strong racial prejudice.

Irrespective of individual attitudes towards the people, the whole atmosphere of missions and settlements was one of paternalism. There was no question of the Aboriginal people being treated as equals or having any meaningful rights or decision making powers. Local councils of Aboriginals were formed at some settlements but they were given no meaningful authority.

It is with this background and in this atmosphere that a new Australian Government policy of self determination has belatedly been promulgated in the last three years. The resilience of the Aboriginal people is demonstrated by the fact that during these long years of institutionalisation not only have they been able to hold onto much of their own social structure and religion but also by the determination they are showing, despite lack of preparation, in their response to the challenge of self determination.

4
THE RETURN

By June, 1975 well in excess of 300 Western Desert people had left Ernabella, Amata and Warburton settlements to live once again in their own country in the Tomkinson Ranges. What has motivated this return? What type of life style do these people aspire to? Can these new communities be sustained?

The answers to these questions may well be vital in determining the future of these local settlements and indeed in determining the future of Australian Aboriginals as a culturally identifiable people.

It is important to all Aboriginal people as this same decentralisation initiative has been taken by Aboriginal groups at missions and settlements throughout the Northern Territory, Western Australia and to a lesser extent in Queensland.

Coombs (1973:14-18) reviews these decentralisation trends by the Pitjantjatjara and also the Pintubi at Papunya, the Bardi at One Arm Point and several groups at Maningrida. In addition to this and since August, 1973 when Coombs wrote, local communities have been initiated by people who have left Yirrkala (N.T.), Oenpelli (N.T.), Mowanjum (W.A.), Mapoon (Queensland) and Elcho Island (N.T.) and other areas.

Coombs concludes "that the decentralisation trend is an Aboriginal response to the problems which contact with white society has created for them". I propose to examine this proposition in relation to the Tomkinson Range people and to offer some tentative conjectures towards answers to the three questions posed above.

In attempting to establish why the people left the settlements it is difficult (as Coombs also points out) to separate fact from conjecture. The invariable response received in answer to this question was simply "this is my country" (ngayaku ngura) and said in such a way as to imply that it was a silly question and where else would they want to live. Traditionally it was for the Pitjantjatjara as Strehlow (1970:135) pointed out for the Aranda, "the totemic landscape formed a firm basis for religion, for the social order and for established order itself".

It becomes conjecture to assess how strong the totality of the man/landscape tie still is and what part this has played in motivating the return. More relevant is the part it will play in sustaining the return in the face of inevitable economic pressures. This total relationship between the local group and its totemic sites is still extremely strong and now that access to vehicles is possible, has provided the over-riding incentive for the people to return and remain on their lands.

A contrary view has been expressed by Capp (personal communication). He suggests the people are concerned with ownership and title to the land and that if this were assured they would be content to only visit their sites occasionally for ritual purposes. Whilst some of the people are very well aware of the necessity to protect their ownership legally particularly in relation to potential mineral or oil exploration, I tend to disagree with this view and will cite some examples which demonstrate the strength of the man/site relationship.

Kunamatta is an isolated mountain about 110 kilometres south-west of Amata. It is the totemic home of the *ili* (fig) totem people and contains several sites of great significance to this local group, particularly a large grove of fig trees and a series of rockholes which are on the path of the ancestral *wati malu*. In june 1974 five elderly Pitjantjatjara who are the owners of the site begged me to take them back there. There were no facilities at Kunamatta except a small shed, a *wiltja* and a bore with a hand pump some 200 metres away (see plate 4:1). Their joy at being back in their own country was demonstatively obvious and these five old people stayed there for several months until problems of maintaining food supplies forced them to return. However, this was the third or fourth time they had done this in the last two years. Despite lack of facilities and lack of a more viable group including some more active younger men they were continually expressing their desire and determination to live in their own country.

Before my visit in February, 1975 the problems associated with a permanent return to Kunamatta had been discussed amongst all the members of this local group which would number in excess of 100 individuals. I use the term local group to mean simply those men and women who identify themselves with this location and express a strong desire to return to it. A key area of further research will be to determine the actual social and ritual basis of their claims on the location and their concept of group membership and identity.

During my visit a meeting of many of these people was organised. The recurring theme of the discussions was the statement of desire by the men to return to live in their own country to look after their sacred sites and to be able to show and teach the younger men about them. Another recurring statement was to mention by name each of the white men to whom they had shown and explained these sacred sites over the last ten years or more and to ask why these men had not repaid this act by getting facilities provided for the people to stay there. It was probably not fully appreciated by the recipients that the act of showing these sites to them was a highly significant act in itself but was also a gift of great value, and a gift which carried with it a reciprocal obligation. It was also realised that the demand for reciprocity had not perhaps been made to the right sources and an approach was made to the Government for funds to expedite the return to Kunamatta. The concept of reciprocal demand giving obligations had been applied to relations between Aboriginals and Europeans. Hamilton (1972:41-45) discusses in some depth the importance in the development of black/white relationships of the repeated attempts of Aboriginals to apply their own kinship based moral code of generosity to Europeans. As she summarises (page 45) "The Aborigines have passed from one means to another; they have provided sexual services, economic services and are now trying to give their ultimate possession, their spiritual knowledge; all the time at every step trying to get the whites to behave morally, properly and generously".

The other example which suggests the strength of the peoples desire to return and renew the permanent links with their local group's sites concerns the return of the *malu* (kangaroo) totem people to sites in the Tomkinson Ranges. A small group first went west towards the end of 1971 and set up a camp at Puta Puta, 190 kilometres from Amata (see figure 1). The mainstays of this group were older men whose totemic sites were in that area. At that stage there were no facilities whatsoever at Puta Puta beyond a bore with a hand pump. The group was dependent on pension money and stores being brought from Amata. However, their life was by no means easy and at the end of March 1974 there were still 30 people at Puta Puta but they had run out of stores and there was no game to hunt. As a group they decided to walk back to Amata but were met on the way by the stroes truck and went straight beack to Puta Puta. Because of abnormally heavy rains they were completely cut off from Amata and supplies. In May 1974 most of the people walked 50 kilometres further west to Wingelina where later they received supplies from Warburton. Two of the very old men, with their wives, walked over 130 kilometeres back towards Amata before being picked up. They had no food or rifle and lived on the rabbit they caught on the ways. As soon as the road was negoitable these two men, plus about 30 others including women and children moved back to their Tomkinson Range

country. At first they joined a larger group at Pipalyatjara 24 kilometres west of Puta Puta then a smaller group of older men, the traditional owners, moved back to Puta Puta area where they are still. The repeated expression by members of this group, of desire to be back in their own countary and close to their sacred sites, has been verified by their action in doing just that in the face of considerable hardship.

The movement of the Tomkinson Range people back to their homeland is gathering momentum. From the initial movement to the larger camp at Pipalyatjara some groups have formed smaller camps at Blackstone, Wingellina and Nyumbantja. Whilst the existence of a bore at each of these locations makes it possible for the groups to exist, it is also true that each of these camps is adjacent to sites of particular significance to the local group. Discussion and observation of the actions of men in the presence of the actual sacred rocks and features of the landscape, indicates that belief in ancestral transformations and the associated ancestral myths of creation remain strong and intact.

I am therefore convinced both from the evidence of the strength of this religious tie between man and landscape and from evidence of the persistent and repeated return of groups to their homeland sites that the principal motivation for this return is what could be termed an act of religious faith.

In suggesting a religious base as the underlying motive for the return I am in no way denying the probability that a whole range of additional interwoven motivations led an individual or a group to take this step. Indeed, given the cultural preconceptions of the observer and the difficulty of meaningful philosophical communication, it would be foolish to be dogmatic on such a complex subject. Coombs (1973: 14-18) reported that in his discussions with these same people they placed overwhelming emphasis on the desire to guard and protect their sacred sites as the reason for their return. Whilst this supports the view of the continued importance of the man/landscape relationship, and protection against intrusion is consequently a vital part of this relationship, the motivation is still much deeper than guardianship.

The other recurring motivational themes that Coombs found amongst all decentralised groups were questions of social cohesion and control and concern about black/white contacts. Whilst I found as did Coombs that these did not appear to be as important to the Pitjantjatjara as they were to other groups, nevertheless these factors are emerging as important in relation to the more relevant question posed earlier concerning the long term viability of the decentralised groups who have returned to their own country.

Whether or not the initiative of these Pitjantjatjara groups in returning to their homeland succeeds and the decentralised settlements survive, in the way the people themselves wish them to survive, cannot be determined by them alone. The outcome will largely rest on the actions of and the nature of, their interaction with Australian Society as a whole. The problem is complex and there are no ready answers. I therefore propose to report some of the problems the people in these groups are facing, how they are meeting these problems and suggest some directional policies aimed at giving support to this initiative.

Plate 5.1:1 Decentralised camp at Pipalyatjara in the Tomkinson Ranges, January 1975. Many Pitjantjatjara people have abandoned the life of the settlement for the freedom of camp-life.

The following sections provide an outline of the material culture and way of life of a small decentralised group of Western Pitjantjatjara people in the Tomkinson Ranges during January-February 1975.

5.1   LOCATION AND ENVIRONMENT

The camp is called Pipalyatjara (see plate 5.1:1) which means literally "by the Pipalya tree". It is the name the people have given to their community. The actual location is at the mouth of a long, narrow valley in the midst of the Tomkinson Ranges 25 kilometres south-east of the junction of the W.A.–N.T.–S.A. borders called Warulkulpa which means "rain place". Water is supplied by a bore and hand pump. The camp is serviced from Amata settlement 220 kilometres to the east over a poor dirt road impassable after heavy rain whilst the nearest habitations to the north and west are Giles Meteorological station (210 kilometres) and Warburton Settlement (350 kilometres) respectively. It is thus an extremely isolated location (see figure 1).

Pipalyatjara has an elevation of 600 metres above sea level being located in the centre of an elevated plateau which extends from the Warburton Ranges in the west to the Everard Ranges in the east. The surrounding mountains rise steeply 300 to 450 metres above the intermontaine valleys which give way to the typical desert complex of long parallel sand dunes 25 kilometres to the South.

There is no permanent natural water in the area although in good seasons it is obtained from soaks in the sandy beds of the ephemeral creeks which criss-cross the valleys or less reliably from natural rockholes at the foot of the mountains.

The vegetation in the valleys is normally sparse consisting mainly of scattered mulga *(Acacia aneura)* corkwood *(Hakea suberea)* desert oak *(Casuarina decaisnea)* trees with mulga or silver grass *(anthistinia)* as the most persistent grass. The larger creeks contain magnificent specimens of river red gum *(Eucalyptus camaldulensis)* which is the *Pipalya* tree from which the community derives its name. In the sand dune country the predominant vegetation is the spinifex bush *(Triodia basedonii)*.

Because of the exceptionally high rainfall in 1974 of 750mm, early in 1975 the valleys abounded in wild flowers *(Helipterum floribundum, Rutidosis helichrysoldes, Ailotus atriplicifolius, Helichrysum apiculatum, Calandria baloncusis)* and a number of plants from which the people gathered edible seeds, roots and berries. The list of these given below is only a fraction of the known Aboriginal food plant resources of the area (see Cleland 1966:111-158) but records those plant foods the Pipalyatjara people showed an   interest in collecting and eating during my stay with them.

The climate of the area with its extremes of temperature has been described earlier. At Pipalyatjara the extreme heat in summer is intensified by its position surrounded by rocky mountains.

Pitjantjatjara Name	Botanical Name	Description and Use
Kaltu Kaltu	Panicum decompositum	Grass seeds ground into flour to make traditional damper
Wangunu	Eragrostis eriopoda	
Wakati	Portulaca oleracea	
Wintalka	Acacia kempeana	Seeds of witchetty bush used as above
Wituka	Beorhavia diffusa	Plant tubers eaten raw or roasted
Tjanmata	Cyperus bulbosus	
Kampurarpa	Solanum centrale	Native tomato eagerly sought and eaten raw
Ili	Ficus platypoda	Native fig eaten raw
Mingkulpa	Nicotiana gossei Nicotiana excelsior	Native tobacco
Ngantjaa	Lysiana murrayi	Small orange berries of the Mulga Mistletoe vine eaten raw

Plate 5.2:1 Young children learn to collect food and enjoy the freedom of camp-life. Camp at Pipalyatjara, January 1975.

Plate 5.2:2 Typical shelter constructed of timber and brush and weather-proofed with tarpaulins. Pipalyatjara camp, January 1975.

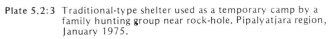

Plate 5.2:3 Traditional-type shelter used as a temporary camp by a family hunting group near rock-hole. Pipalyatjara region, January 1975.

5.2   THE CAMP AND SHELTER

In January 1975 there were only 33 people in the camp. This was composed of four couples with 11 of their children aged between 1 and 15, four old couples without their children, three old women whose husbands were away and three young unmarried men. The camp consisted of 16 shelters or *wiltjas* arranged in a roughly circular pattern about 10 metres apart (see plate 5.2:1). Each *wiltja* contained the basic family unit of a man, his wife and children if they were in the camp. The three young men lived in one shelter.

The shelters ranged in size from 1.5m by 1.5m to 3m by 2.5m and the height from 1.2m to 1.8m. The uniform construction consisted of a loose framework of tree limbs over which was placed a covering of brush and in most instances this was covered with a tarpaulin (plate 5.2:2). Three of the family groups had an open sided shade shelter adjacent to the sleeping *wiltja* which was used during the day. The roofs are used to store food away from the reach of dogs.

To European eyes these simple shelters may appear offensive and hundreds of thousands of dollars have been wasted in the investigation, design and construction of "special" and "transitional" houses for Aboriginals on settlements which in many cases are not used. Two observations can be made in respect of the Pitjantjatjara: Firstly, where a family choose to live in a large and static community with permanent employment there is no reason why they should not aspire to and be able to live in exactly the same type of house as Europeans on the settlement, certainly this is now happening at Ernabella. Secondly, the people who choose to live in small remote groups, like Pipalyatjara, should be allowed to determine the type of shelter that they themselves want. At present they are trying tents and some are attracted to caravans both of which fit the requirement of mobility.

Some groups may well decide that the traditional *wiltja* of boughs and bush is most suitable for the climate as well as giving the ability to move around their estate. Plate 5.2:3 is a traditional type *wiltja* built by an old couple who left Pipalyatjara and stayed for a short period at Kunatjara rockhole some 25 kilometres away.

5.3   MATERIAL POSSESSIONS

When early explorers like Basedow (1904:24) encountered the nomadic Pitjantjatjara they commented on the sparcity of their material possessions. For the men the spear thrower and spears, for the women wooden carrying bowls, a digging stick and grinding stones exhausted their list. Whilst the character of the possessions of the Pipalyatjara people has changed the range has increased very little as the list given below indicates.

- For hunting — most men own a rifle with .22 calibre repeater being most popular.

- For fighting — the older men particularly, retain their traditional spear thrower and three long spears *(kulata)* as well as a short stabbing spear *(winta)*.

- For food gathering — for digging out rabbits and lizards the women possess an iron crowbar *(karupa)* a shovel *(tjapala)* and a flat steel dish hammered out of a car hubcap.

For carrying berries or fruits a billycan is used and for carrying water a two to four gallon tin or plastic container.

- For food preparation — a billycan for tea making is universal with occasionally some enamel mugs. Some women possess a large flat iron pot for making damper from flour and one or two women still have grindstones.

- For food storage — one or two five gallon openhead drums with lids are most general.

- For warmth — generally each family possesses up to three or four blankets.

- For clothing — after the age of about eight all the people remain fully clothed during the day, the men long trousers and a shirt, the women a long dress. The old women particularly possess and wear up to four or five dresses at once, even in the middle of summer merely putting a new acquisition over the previous ones. Crocheted woollen berets are a popular head-dress with the men and women. The younger men wear cowboy type hats and boots whilst the men and women will wear boots and shoes if given to them but often discard them and revert to bare feet.

- For manufacturing artifacts — the traditional stone tools have been completely replaced by metal tools comprising axe, tomahawk, rasp and a modified adzing tool made from an old chisel welded to a piece of ½" pipe from 0.5m to 1m long and small chisels for incising designs.

- For recreation — the young children possess marbles and a few teenagers a battery cassette player and a supply of country and western tapes.

The changes that have occurred in material possessions and their function, can be summarised as follows:

Completely new items —
blankets and clothing, the billycan which enables water to be heated to make tea.

Major substitutions —
the rifle in place of the spear thrower and spear and the axe and tomahawk in place of hand-held stone axe as there is no evidence to date that stone axes in this area were either edge-ground or hafted.

Substitutions of material only —
as will be discussed in more detail later all the other items are a substitution of steel tools for stone tools for cutting shaping or grinding and the substitutions of steel for wood for carrying storage or digging.

5.4   DAILY LIFE — DIVISION OF LABOUR

My presence in the camp obviously skewed the people's daily routine towards assisting me in my pursuits and also making best use of me and my truck. Even if one wished it courtesy and reciprocal obligations to ones hosts would make the playing of the role of unobtrusive and disinterested observer untenable. With this proviso the daily life of the Pipalyatjara is summarised below.

The sexual division of labour is quite clear and is still broadly that the men hunt and indulge in ceremonial activities whilst the women gather and prepare vegetable foods and small lizards, marsupials and rabbits.

Plate 5.4:1   For Pitjantjatjara hunters the rifle has replaced the
spear and spear thrower. Tomkinson Ranges,
January 1975.

Women's activities are more ordered and arduous than the mens. First they have the task which is performed once or twice each day, of pumping water from the bore and transporting it to camp, a distance of about 250 metres (see plates 5.4:2, 5.4:3). The women carry the water on their heads in tins or plastic containers of 9 to 14 litre capacity. A piece of cloth substitutes the traditional circular woven hair and fur head ring *(manguri)* — see plate 6.5:4. On one occasion one of the women carried a 23 litre jerrycan, with a total weight of 24 kg, in this fashion although she did complain afterwards that she was *katapika* (headache). This activity consumes between one and two hours per day for each of the adult women although the children give some assistance on occasions.

Plate 5.4:2   Availability of a regular supply of water is essential to
sustain life in the desert. This hand-pump and bore at
Pipalyatjara has been replaced by a windmill and tank.

Plate 5.4:3   The day's water supply being carried from the bore to
the camp. This is a regular task of the women.
Pipalyatjara, January 1975.

The men obviously derive great enjoyment and satisfaction from hunting and prefer this activity to anything else. The rifle has completely replaced the spear thrower and spear (plate 5.4:1). In order of preference the men hunted kangaroos, emus, scrub turkeys and rabbits. In January-February 1975 as none of this game, apart from rabbits, was present near the camp, it was often necessary to drive up to 30 to 50 kilometres from the camp in search of game. If kangaroos or emu were sighted in terrain impassable for a vehicle the men would stalk them on foot up to 15 kilometres or so. Many times they were unsuccessful due to the inaccuracy of their rifles but this did in no way dampen the men's ardour for hunting. A major men's activity was making new sacred boards *(kulpitja)*. Two large boards took four men two days of unceasing work to complete. Another men's activity which was to some extent stimulated and increased by the writer's presence, was the manufacture of artifacts which will be discussed in detail in later sections. Here again there is a clear sexual dichotomy with the men making only weapons; spears; spear throwers, shields and boomerangs, whilst the women make wooden bowls, animal carvings and other adapted craft.

Amongst the men there is little specialisation of activity. Except for some of the younger men who are disinterested, all make artifacts although some are more adept and energetic in this task than others. The old men do not hunt when they have failing eyesight. The young, initiated men are not generally involved in making sacred boards. Because the ingredients of the main men's activities, that is, game to hunt and wood to fashion weapons, are available only beyond walking distance of the camp. the men's activities are not ordered but are regulated by the chance availability of a vehicle. An alternative, although much less desired, tinned food is mostly available; hunting is not a necessity for survival but if food is short the people will, as one man and wife did during my stay, wander away for short periods and resume a nomadic existence in search of game.

The other women's tasks are assisting with collection of firewood, such food preparation as is carried out, the manufacture of artifacts, which will be dealt with later in this report, the gathering of fruits, berries, and grubs when available and finally their most regular and time consuming activity, searching out and digging up rabbits for food.

Rabbits have been present in the Tomkinson Ranges and have been a source of food for the Pitjantjatjara, for a considerable period. Basedow (1904:15) noted their presence in 1904 and remarked that they were a welcome and easily attained source of meat. They are still a welcome and indeed a major source of food for the Pitjantjatjara people but are attained only by means of arduous almost daly effort by the women. As the nearby burrows have been worked out, the women walk up to 15 kilometes from the camp carrying their rabbiting tool kit of crowbar and shovel, in search of fresh burrows. These are readily located from evidence of recent tracks and dung. The length of a likely burrow is traced out by probing with a crowbar (plate 5.4:4) which is also used to determine the presence of a rabbit. The burrow in then literally dug up (plate 5.4:5) until the rabbit is within arms length (plate 5.4:6) when it is extracted and killed by stretching its neck (plate 5.4:7). The rabbits are gutted, the abdominal cavity stuffed with rabbit fur and sealed with a mulga twig. During my stay with the people this hard physical work was carried out in the sun in temperatures of well over 40°C for several hours almost each day without complaint. The catch for this effort which consumed up to five hours per day, varied between one and five rabbits per woman and provided the bulk of the people's meat supply.

At Pipalyatjara the daily routine of the women was as follows; arise before dawn, kindle fire, make tea, work on artifact manufacture for an hour or so, collect water and leave on a rabbiting excursion in mid-morning. Return late afternoon, collect wood and water, have a meal, then work on artifacts until dark.

Plate 5.4:5 The arduous task of digging out the burrows is left to the women.

Plate 5.4:6 The rabbit is pulled from the burrow.

Plate 5.4:7 Killing the rabbit by breaking its neck.

Apart from helping to pump water or gather wood occasionally, the children were not called on to perform regular chores and spent most days happily playing as a group. A favourite pastime was what we refer to as "knucklebones" using marbles or stones (plate 5.4:9) or singing songs which were mostly Pitjantjatjara versions of English songs learnt at Amata school. The following was sung to the tune of Round and Round the Mulberry Bush:

Manguri manguri para pitja
Round and Round we go

para pitja parapitja
round and round

mungawinki kula
at school in the morning

It is interesting to note how English words have been modified into the Pitjantjatjara phonetic such as school = *kula* and crowbar = *karupa*.

Another activity involving both men and women is the time spent on communications amongst the group. During the day this involved continuous movement between the *wiltjas* of those in the camp but it was during the evening and occasionally just before dawn that total camp discussion was carried on. Although the *wiltjas* were laid out in a rough circle with a radius of about 25 metres these discussions were carried on sometimes for as long as two hours without the participants leaving their own hearth. The men particularly have remarkable powers of oratory, effortlessly using all the orators skills of changes in volume, inflexion and tone as well as repetition and all this to an audience up to 25 or 30 metres away. These discussions often became most animated and even verbally violent but during my stay at least, never led to violence or fighting. It would appear on the surface that this is a rather elegant social device that enabled people to give vent to emotions and test group opinion on issues under a fabricated cloak of distance and anonyminity although the voices of the actors were of course well known to each other.

Three factors stand out from observance of the daily life of the Pipalyatjara group at that time.

Firstly the men and women were active and busy for most of the day, whether the men were hunting, chopping wood for or actually fashioning weapons or sacred boards or whether the women were digging rabbit burrows or making artifacts they went about their task with sustained vigour despite the searing summer heat. The only exception to this was the three young men in the camp who were rather excluded from the normal activities and were much less active.

Secondly at that time almost all the men's and women's activities were modified forms of their traditional hunting and gathering roles. Whilst the amount of time spent on each activity, and the methods and the equipment have changed markedly as has been noted, the only new activities introduced were riding in a motor vehicle to a hunting ground instead of walking, pumping water from a bore instead of scooping from a soak or rockhole, washing clothes and making new types of artifacts from wood rather than manufacture and maintenance of basic weapons and utensils.

Thirdly all these activities, many of which as described were arduous and tedious, were carried out in a most cheerful and happy manner. An observer could only describe the atmosphere and demeanour of the people as happy and relaxed despite an occasional quarrel. It could be conjectured that this atmosphere is in some manner related to the small size of the group, the absence of Europeans with any authority and most likely the productive and creative nature of most of the daily activities.

However, this whole pattern is now undergoing considerable change. At the end of the writer's stay at Pipalyatjara the people received their own truck, a European mining adviser joined them to assist to carry out small mining activities and sheds and windmills were being built. These desirable facilities which had been requested by the community, will also present them with a whole new set of circumstances which will affect their way of life.

Plate 5.4:9 Despite few material possessions children amuse themselves happily. "Knucklebones" played with stones and marbles is a popular past-time. Pipalyatjara, 1975.

5.5 FOOD

Food is obtained from two sources: by purchase for cash from the supply truck which normally came out from Amata settlement every two weeks and from hunting and gathering. Both the range and quantity of foods from both sources were a variable. The food purchased depended on the goods the storekeeper loaded on the truck and the money the people had to purchase them. The food obtained by hunting and gathering depended both on the skill of the Aboriginals and the season.

Within these variables there were certain foods consistently available which formed the basis of the people's diet whilst others were less regularly available as shown in the table below.

The irregular availability of certain purchased foods was due mainly to lack of funds for the people to purchase sufficient quantity for two weeks, lack of suitable storage facilities and a custom to consume these items rapidly after the arrival of the store truck. No attempt is made to quantify or assess dietry value of food intake as this could be misleading without detailed monitoring and expert assessment which was impossible. However, it would appear that there may be some dietary deficiencies and expert advice as well as educational efforts should be made available to the community in a sustained manner.

In general terms hunting and gathering provided about 80% of the meat intake and something less than 5% of the vegetable food. The utilisation of gathered vegetable foods was limited by the effort and time involved in having to walk longer and longer distances from the camp to collect them as nearer sources were exhausted and in certain instances in having to prepare the foods when a readily available sub-stitute, prepared food, was available. Because of this latter reason traditional damper made from the seeds of *kaltu kaltu (Panicum decompositum)* was rarely used in place of white flour, damper made from which was a staple food.

At my request some of the women did collect *kaltu kaltu* and prepare traditional damper from it which indicates the technology is still well known and could be readily used in an emergency.

Briefly the method is as follows. The small (of the order of 1mm diameter) black, oily seeds are contained in spear-shaped pods along the wispy stems of the grass *Panicum decompositum* which are wrenched off the mainstems (plate 5.5:1). These stems are then crushed by hand into a container and a proportion of the straw discarded (plate 5.5:2). The chaff so formed is separated by winnowing (plate 5.5:3). The mixture of fine chaff and seeds is transferred to a *kanilypa* (made from a flattened car hubcap) where by a most skilful process in which the *kanilypa* is oscillated rapidly about its long axis combined with a slower see-sawing motion and an occasional sharp bump using the knee, the seed moves to one end of the *kanilypa* and the chaff to the other (plate 5.5:4). The seeds are then mixed with water (plate 5.5:5) placed on a flat lower grinding stone *(tjiwa)* and worked into a paste by imparting pressure as well as a rolling and oscillating movement to a rounded top grinding stone *(tjungari)* (plate 5.5:6). The paste is shaped into a flat pat and placed in the ashes of a fire for about 20 minutes (plate 5.5:7) and is then ready to eat (plate 5.5:8). The completed product *(nyuma)* has a most pleasant if slightly gritty taste and judging by the mad scramble of the children for a piece was considered something of an unusual treat.

That it is not regularly made is not surprising as the time and labour involved is considerable. Although *kaltu kaltu* was plentiful within a kilometre of the camp it took three women three hours working steadily to collect and return to camp with what finished up to be less than 2kg of seed. Grinding and baking took another two hours for one woman with the end result two dampers about 20 cm × 15 cm × 3 cm in size.

Pipalyatjara – January 1975

Range of Foods Utilised

Frequency	Purchased Foods	Obtained from Hunting and Gathering
Eaten practically all the time	White flour Tea Sugar	Rabbits
Eaten irregularly or for short periods only	Tinned meat Biscuits Tinned fruit Jam Soft Drink Fruit juice Fresh Fruit	Kangaroo Emu Bush turkey Lizards Witchetty grubs *Kampurarpa* (wild tomato)

Plate 5.5:1-8 Prior to European contact damper made from grass-seeds was a basic element of the diet. Mabel Bryant prepares traditional damper at Pipalyatjara in January, 1975.

Plate 5.5:1 Seed-pods of the grass *Panicum decompositum* are gathered. Aboriginal women are highly skilled at food preparation.

Plate 5.5:2 Crushing the stems into a container so that the surplus can be discarded.

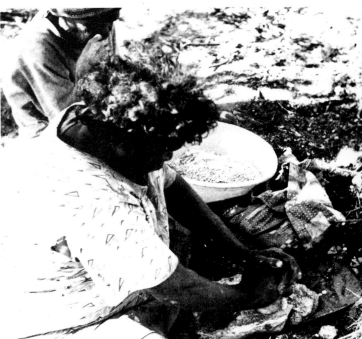

Plate 5.5:5 Mixing seeds with water on a flat slab of sand-stone known as the lower grinding stone.

Plate 5.5:6 A top stone grinder is used to grind the mixture into a fine paste.

Plate 5.5:3 Winnowing to separate the seeds from the lighter pieces of chaff.

Plate 5.5:4 Separating grass seeds from the remaining chaff by oscillation of the bowl *kanilypa* is a skilful process.

Plate 5.5:7 Damper is baked in the ashes in the age-old method.

Plate 5.5:8 Seed damper was a highly prized and nutritious food.

Plate 5.5:9   Fruits, nuts and berries have always been an important food
supplement for the Pitjantjatjara people. A group of women
and children collect native tomatoes *kampurarpa* in the
Tomkinson Ranges, January 1975.

Plate 5.5:10 Witchetty grubs (larvae of *bupestrid* beetles) are a prized
and nutritious delicacy. The grubs are found in the roots
of the bush *Acasia kempeana.*

The other foods collected by the women were so-called "native tomato" kampurarpa *(Solanum centrale)* with its small (1 to 2 cm diameter) slightly sour but pleasant fruit which is eagerly sought, collected and eaten raw by men, women and children (see plate 5.5:9). At this time of year *maku* or witchetty grubs (larvae of *buprestid* beetles) were plentifully available from the roots of the witchetty bush *(Acacia kempeana).* They were obtained by digging down with the ubiquitous *karupa,* breaking open the soft roots and extracting the grub by hand (plate 5.5:10). Collecting for an hour or so could yield two or three pounds of this delicacy (plate 5.5:11) which is eaten raw or very lightly cooked.

Whilst bush foods provided quantitatively only a small proportion of the diet not only was the opportunity to hunt or gather *Kampurarpa* or witchetty grubs eagerly sought but the foods so obtained were preferred to purchased goods.

This applied particularly to the men's desire to hunt and eat game. The method of butchering and cooking kangaroo was identical to the method described by Gould (1967:41-66) and will not be repeated here except to add one observation. It was stated to be strictly taboo for women to eat any portion of the tail. This difference may be due to the fact that the kangaroo is the "cult" totem (Elkin 1968:179-180) of the people concerned.

The people themselves will not allow alcohol to be consumed in the camp or anywhere on their tribal lands. This rule is policed by the Aboriginal councils with the support of the community who are aware of the problems caused by excessive alcohol consumption at Alice Springs and at other settlements. Apart from some of the younger men, few of the men and none of the women smoke to any extent but many of the men and women chew native tobacco *(mingkulpa).* Two species *Nicotiana gossei* and *Nicotiana excelsior* are in common use.

The method of preparation of *mingkulpa* is shown in plates 5.5:12-14. The leaves of the *Nicotiana* bush, after picking, are crunched into a small heap and rolled in the ashes of Mulga needles *(Acacia aneura)* which according to Cleland (1966: 120) facilitates the liberation of the narcotic by the alkali in the ash. The ash from the bark of the *Pipalya* tree *(Eucalyptus camaldulensis)* was stated to be also used for the same purpose. The ball of native tobacco so formed is carried around between the lips (plate 5.5:15) or behind the ear.

Plate 5.5:11 Wichetty grubs are eaten raw or lightly roasted in a fire.

Plate 5.5:12 Native tobacco *mingkulpa* is widely used by both men and women. One species *Nicotiana gossei* being picked in the Musgrave Ranges.

Plate 5.5:13 The ash of the needles of the Mulga tree is added to the crushed green leaves of the native tobacco so that the nicotine is released.

Plate 5.5:14 The mulga ash and the tobacco leaves are mixed and
rolled into a ball.

Plate 5.5:15 The finished product is usually held between the lips.

5.6   ECONOMY

Apart from a small subsistence contribution from hunting and gathering, the Pitjantjatjara people operate in a cash economy. Cash is received from social service payments and the sale of artifacts. Significant income was also derived from the mining of chrysoprase up to three or four years ago and is now being recommenced. The income so received was spent on purchase of European goods from the stores truck mainly food as well as items such as clothing, blankets, patent medicines and tools.

On the surface therefore it would appear appropriate to quantify this level of income, to analyse how it is expended and then compare these with other sections of the Australian community so that statements can be made about relative income and standard of living. However, to do this is to make the assumption that Western economic organisation is automatically applicable which leads to further assumptions that it is not only right but inevitable that these groups of Aboriginal people should progress in the Western economic mode. As acceptance of these assumptions is implicit in current Government policies in Aboriginal affairs in the use of terms such as improving standards of living and developing viable commercial enterprises, it is relevant to examine and question their validity.

To do this it is helpful to look at a historical perspective. From the observations of early explorers and ethnographers it would appear a reasonable assumption that the Pitjantjatjara moved around this countryside living by a subsistence economy based on hunting and gathering. Whilst we cannot be sure how the groups and territories were organised we can assume that their movements were dictated by the seasons and availability of water, game and vegetable foods and that these movements may have been far ranging. We could also assume from the current climatic records that for a few centuries at least the climate varied in a similar way so that in some years food and water were plentiful in others scarce and the effort of both movement and food collection varied. We can even take some of these assumptions back in time with some surety from the work of Gould (1968:161-185) who concluded from the evidence of excavation at Puntutjarpa rock shelter in the Warburton Ranges that "It is a site with at least 6,700 years of uninterrupted cultural history culminating in the present day Ngatatjara Aboriginals. The economy was at all times based on hunting and gathering with changes mainly in the relative dependence on different staples" (p.180).

When we move on from assumptions about the way of life to assumptions about the economic quality of life of pre-contact Western Desert people we are reduced to little more than conjecture for as Gould (1960:265) points out, there has been no opportunity to make sustained observations of nomadic Aboriginals under severe drought conditions.

Meggitt (1968:24) records that in the drought of 1924-1929, after the first two years, few Walbiri dared to remain in the central desert and a number perished whilst the rest were forced to seek food from the white men who in this area, had more intensively affected their area with cattle stations and prospecting camps than was the case with the Pitjantjat-

jara lands. This is a post-contact situation so we are still left with conjecture about the pre-contact situation except to surmise that the people experienced periods of hardship, but there is no evidence to support a view that the people lived a continuously precarious existence on the borders of starvation.

Sahlins (1968:85-89, 1974:1-39) extends this notion to suggest that hunter-gatherers were the "original affluent society". He defines an affluent society as one in which all the peoples material wants are easily satisfied and suggests from admittedly the limited evidence available that many hunter-gatherer societies were able to satisfy their food requirements and modest items of material culture without having to work hard and continuously leaving them plenty of time to spare. It is not proposed to repeat Sahlins arguments (see Sahlins 1974:1-39) or his analysis of the work of McCarthy and McArthur in Arnhem Land (see McCarthy and McArthur 1960) but to examine the applicability of his general proposition to explain the observed attitudes and habits of the present day Western Pitjantjatjara.

This general proposition then is that hunter-gatherers were able to easily satisfy their wants and they under used their economic possibilities without straining their labour and material resources. Further it is suggested that hunter-gatherers were for these reasons in general happy contented people (see Lee and DeVore 1968:89-95).

The contrasting economic mode described by Sahlins is Western industrial society which he describes as " . . . dedicated to the proposition of scarcity with man the prisoner at hard labour of a perpetual disparity between unlimited wants and insufficient means . . .". A one sentence summary hardly does justice to our Western economic system but it is sufficient for our purpose which is to outline the extent of change in economic philosophy which Aboriginal groups are expected by most administrations to wish to make.

My proposition is that we cannot assume that Aboriginal groups want to make this change *in toto* and my observations of the Pipalyatjara people tend to support this view. Whilst the people were only able to supply a very small part of their food requirements by hunting and gathering nevertheless it was together with artifact manufacture the "work" they elected to do. As we postulated for pre-contact times it was an activity that allowed time for leisure and could be performed intermittedly. Likewise no storage of these foods was attempted and game or fruits were completely consumed.

As the religious and social philosophies of the people have been largely retained (as will be briefly discussed in a later section) so the economic hunter-gatherer philosophy of the people has to an extent remained. This could in part be due to the people looking from their historical viewpoint not only what acceptance of Western economic philosophy can give them but also what it takes away from them. The obvious things it takes away are freedoms. The freedom of more leisure, the freedom to work intermittently at a pace necessary to meet immediate wants, the freedom to work at tasks which are immediately rewarding, the freedom of mobility and the freedom to spend extended periods at appropriate times of the year in religious activities.

At Pipalyatjara it was evident from the patterns of the people's activities, and the people's repeated affirmations of their satisfaction with this way of life that these freedoms which they still enjoyed, were highly prized. But as will be discussed in the final section of this paper both the people's aspirations for some Western goods and their place in the context of the total Australian society limit their range of choices. However, there may be other alternatives than the complete adoption of the Western industrial economic system.

It is perhaps superfluous to add that some of the strains and disillusionments evident in Western societies arise from people's problems in trying to bridge the gap between means and wants and at the same time aspiring to enjoy some of the freedoms which were enjoyed by hunter-gatherer societies.

As mentioned at the beginning of this section the economics of remote groups of Aboriginals should be looked at in much broader terms than analysis of cash income and expenditure. However, it is part of the means-end equation and the average income and form of expenditure for the Pipalyatjara group in early 1975 was as follows:

■ The main source of income was social service payments which varied from approximately $30 per week for old age pensioners to $73 per week for unemployment benefits for two of the men with a wife and four children to support. Two women in addition received $5 per week child endowment. During this period the men and women actively made artifacts and sold between $200 and $250 worth per week.

■ The average income of the 19 adults was $30 per week from social service payments and $10 per week from artifact sales. This was disposed of roughly in the following manner:

Purchase of food	$20 to $30 per week
Purchase of blankets, bullets, etc.	$ 5 to $10 per week
Saved for vehicles or sent elsewhere to relatives	$10 to $15 per week

These figures are rather meaningless without knowledge of the exact composition of the camp at any time in terms of kinship sharing and support obligations. All the economic transactions at that time were completed in the space of an hour or two once a fortnight when the pensions and stores truck arrived. Pension cheques and artifacts were exchanged for money which was then all virtually exchanged back for the food and supplies brought on the truck.

It is relevant to state that even in the few months since January, 1975 this situation has changed somewhat with the introduction of some "award wages" work around the camp and the setting up of a small store but the end result economically would not be very different.

5.7 MOBILITY

The Pitjantjatjara rate the ability to be mobile high if not at the top of their list of current priorities. As mentioned earlier we could conjecture with a fair degree of certainty that mobility was also vitally important in pre-contact times.

It was important for a whole host of reasons. The main ones being to find food and water to survive, to enable men to obtain wives, to enable small groups to congregate into larger groups for religious ceremonies and to visit sacred places. For these reasons long journeys often lasting weeks and months were made on foot.

Today the desire to be mobile stems from similar reasons — the desire to move around to hunt, to visit relatives, to visit sacred sites and to congregate for ceremonies. To do this the people need motor vehicles which are always on the top of the list of requests to administrators and the prime purchase if money can be saved.

With good reason the motor vehicle is also a coveted status symbol, perhaps the only item of white man's hardware so regarded. The good reason is that during most of the long institutionalisation period it was only Europeans who owned or had the use of vehicles. Aboriginals had to rely on the patronage of friendly Europeans to obtain a lift. The provision of vehicles within the last two years to incorporated Pitjantjatjara groups has enabled some of the people to make their own decisions to move around their land for important social or religious reasons. In January, 1975 over 200 Pitjantjatjara people, using their own community and private vehicles, were able to organise and perform a whole series of important ceremonies over a period of two weeks at appropriate sites stretching for a distance of 300 kilometres from Amata to Blackstone in W.A.

Many Pitjantjatjara men have purchased their own motor cars and the large number (over 100 at Amata) of abandoned cars is suggested by some Europeans as an example of Aboriginal ineptness. It is more an example of European exploitation and laxity. Firstly, because of the strong need for a motor vehicle, often the people will purchase a second-hand vehicle for the minimum amount of money and have been shamelessly exploited by dealers in the towns who sell them cars in a shocking condition knowing full well they will be lucky to make it back to the settlement let alone get any service from the vehicle. Secondly, administrators have been lax in not developing extensive training programs for Aboriginal mechanics. Thirdly, if a car does break down and the driver is unable to fix it he has no recourse but to abandon it as there is no N.R.M.A. to call on and Government mechanics cannot or will not offer any assistance.

For these reasons and because the maintenance of material possessions has not been the mainstay of the people's economic philosophy, as it is in Western society, cars have tended to be things that always break down so one leaves it and saves up for another. Concerted efforts in training and provision of repair facilities could overcome most of these problems as with a minimum of training many of the people have proved to be extraordinarily skilful in vehicle maintenance.

There are problems of a social and political organisational nature in the control of community vehicles but the benefits conferred on the communities by providing vehicles is so great and the need for mobility so high that Governments should respond to the people's wish to continue and increase the provision of vehicles to remote communities, without reacting punitively to instances of misuse, in our terms, during this period of difficult adjustment.

5.8 POLITICAL ORGANISATION AND LEADERSHIP

As discussed previously the Pitjantjatjara and the decentralised communities, such as Pipalyatjara, are faced with the problem of coping with the rate of economic change. Likewise the people are faced with probably a greater problem of developing new or modified forms of political organisation to cope with a whole range of new and changing situations. The problems of leadership and authority particularly are observably placing communities under a great deal of stress.

There appears to have been little specific information gathered in the early contact period about the politics and leadership of the Pitjantjatjara. Gould (1969:90) generalises broadly and somewhat doubtfully about the Western Desert Ngatatjara in the following terms . . . "In daily life there are no official leaders or privileged groups, hereditary or elected among the Aborigines" It would perhaps be truer to say that the types of leadership that we are accustomed to in our society were not present but complex forms of age and ritual gradings to some extent took their place.

No attempt will be made to review or summarise the literature on Aboriginal leadership but some conclusions of Berndt (Law and Order in Aboriginal Australia 1965:167-206) and Meggitt (Forms of Government among Australian Aborigines 1966:57-74) which appear particularly relevant to the present day situation are quoted below.

■ " . . . whatever the composition of the (local) community might be when any situation demanded joint action the programmes that selected the actions and steered their activities to desired ends were more or less standardised and rigid. What men did at that time should have duplicated as far as possible what the ancestors or the culture heroes did on similar occasions in the far past in the Dreamtime." (Meggitt 1966:69).

■ " In these kinds of societies then, where there existed interlocking sets of clearly formulated, publicly accepted and religious sanctioned norms covering all manner of activities, there was little need or room for chiefs or headmen." (Meggitt 1966:71).

■ " . . . "in every response to breaches of one sort or another (against law and order) two dominant pressures are present. The pull of kin is significant in social affairs. Any accusations against or by one person inevitably involved others . . . . The other dominant pressure towards settlement of breaches is tradition itself. Use of precepts from the past as a precedent in determining courses of action in the present is in itself an aspect of control." (Berndt (1965:203-4).

The above quotations do not anywhere near cover the scope of the articles mentioned which should be read in full but they are hopefully sufficiently illustrative for the purposes of this brief discussion.

What then are the new situations facing the Pitjantjatjara people which are causing stresses in the community and problems of leadership and control? The following examples refer only to those situations personally observed and only start to cover a complex and changing problem to which it is hoped much more relevant research effort can be directed.

The situations causing stress are those where the community is required to take some joint action to resolve breaches against new European norms, laws, or expectations about how the community should behave. There were at Pipalyatjara no problems in handling breaches against traditional norms of behaviour. For example, a traditional problem arose over one man making false accusations about another man paying attention to his wife. This was settled traditionally by ritual and reciprocal spearings through the thighs. In Meggitt's terms there was a clearly formulated and publicly accepted norm covering the resolution of this dispute.

A major cause of stress is that communities have been incorporated and as such are given the custody of community property such as trucks. As nomadic hunter-gatherers the local groups had no community property except perhaps the sacred boards (kulpitja) whose care and custody were clearly assigned to certain leaders. If, as happened, a member of the community or one of his close relatives, took the community truck not as was expected to collect stores but off in the opposite direction to visit friends and relatives, there were no precepts from the past to guide the course of action or prescribed sanctions to apply. So no action was taken and this created stresses within the community itself whose members were disadvantaged, and between the community and the administrators who logically expect community property to be used for the benefit of the whole community. However, I would suggest that no action was taken because there was no person or group who had authority to do so.

This is unlike a traditional breach where custom not only laid down the sanctions and the actors who would impose them, but also legitimised the actions as a proper exercise of power. The members of the Council or other mature men who might have taken action were aware that the exercise of what would be considered illegitimate power by the recipient would create much greater intra-community conflict than the inconvenience caused by not taking action themselves apart from perhaps in despair appealing to white authorities.

One could well ask at this point — are there no leaders in the community who can make decisions about such matters as allocation and control of the resources being given to the community and if this is so how can the communities become self determining? There are indeed leaders within the Pipalyatjara community and depending on the manner and degree of European support the communities can in my view be quite self determining.

There are ritual leaders in the group. Meggitt (1966:71) suggested for traditional Aboriginal society that this ritual authority did not extend into secular affairs unless he was a man of exceptional personality or intelligence. The situation is as pointed out no longer entirely governed by traditional norms but the men who now appear to exercise most influence in the community are those who are middle aged, have gained a high degree of ritual status and still have the strength and vigour to be good hunters and debators. The influence of the old men who were ritual leaders was not obvious but I suspect was still strongly and more covertly used. However, in this contact situation other qualifications such as ability to speak some English or to drive a truck confer influence, but a man must be at least a "wati pulka" or a "full man" who has undergone the rites of circumcision, subincision and, the so-called "red ochre" rites to participate in the power structure. Within this group leaders, some of them younger men, are emerging and by their own charisma or intelligence and ability to debate or by force are guiding the community through this period of accelerated and introduced change. Whilst these men have power and influence and many are members of the elected council, as yet there is no real authority structure with prescribed rules to cover these new situations.

5.9 HEALTH AND MEDICINE

No investigations of any medical value were possible with the Pipalyatjara people. Some general observations will be given in regard to the people's approach to health and to the level of health services provided.

Before doing so it is appropriate to quote some health indicators which are available for the total Central Australian Aboriginal Community serviced by the Alice Springs Aero-medical service which includes Amata and Ernabella.

Dr. Kirke (1974:81-87) quotes the following composite data for the years 1964-1971. Life expectancy was 40.2 years at one year of age, and 47.3 years at two years of age (compared with 1960-1962 figures for the whole of Australia of 71.5 years and 70.6 years respectively). Crude death rate was 19.4 deaths per 1,000 of population compared with the 1967 total Australian rate of 8.7. Infant mortality rate was 172 infant deaths per 1,000 live births compared with the 1966 rate for Northern Territory non-aborigines of 19.5. During this period over 50% of all Aboriginal deaths were children under two years of age with the causes of death primarily respiratory infections, diarrhoeal disease and malnutrition. With respect to malnutrition he adds the alarming comment that "nutritional deprivation during the growing period of the human brain is likely to produce reduction in head size and the number of neurones which in turn lowers learning ability".

Given this appalling background what are the indications of the level of health of the Western Pitjantjatjara and what are the attitudes of authorities to the provision of health services which were apparent in the field in early 1975?

There was no provision for trained medical assistance at Pipalyatjara or for visitations on a regular basis. Although since remedied for several long periods the people had no vehicle or radio with the nearest medical sister 220 km away at Amata. The health of the people appeared better than that at the settlement which may well have been due to the fact that they were able to supplement the inadequate stores diet (mainly white flour damper, tea and sugar) with protein from rabbits and occasional kangaroo and some bush foods, like *Kampurarpa* and witchetty grubs which are highly nutritious. The people were energetic and active walking long distances, hunting, rabbiting or collecting bush foods. However, there was a high incidence of eye infections particularly among the older women. There were virtually none of the nose and throat infections characterised by perpetual running noses common in settlement children although many of the younger children had badly infected body sores.

The traditional belief system regarding the causes and cure of illness is still firmly held although superimposed on it now is a realisation that some of the "white feller" ideas about cause and effect of illness and the efficacy of some of his medicines is at least partly accepted.

The traditional beliefs are described by Hamilton (1971:1-18) and will not be repeated here but from what little discussion I was able to have with the people on this subject their beliefs appear to parallel those of the Pitjantjatjara and Yakuntjatjara at Everard Park discussed by Hamilton. In particular the belief that illness is caused by supernatural forces through which a foreign object, which is the root cause of the illness is implanted in the victim's body is found here also.

In the small group at Pipalyatjara there were three tribal doctors *(ngangkari)* now called *"wati doctors"*. If it was apparent that someone was sick the *wati* doctors would automatically attend and give treatment to the patient. The treatment consisted firstly of massage which from close observation was seen to be lengthily and expertly done and appear to parallel those of the Pitjantjatjara and Yankuntjatjara treatments witnessed this was invariably followed by sucking the affected part and removing "bad blood" and the cause of the problem, the foreign object. None of the *"purnu"* or highly polished sticks pointed at both ends mentioned by Hamilton were seen to be extracted. Rather it was generally a more nondescript small piece of dark wood or in one case a piece of razor blade.

With regard to European medicine there was continual demand for such medical treatment as I could offer. Eye drops for eye irritations, the dressing of children's sores as well as cough syrup and aspirin as "cure alls" were regularly dispensed. The acceptance of some European ideas on cause and effect in sickness was perhaps demonstrated by the group's decision to take the unusual step of shooting three exceptionally mangy camp dogs when it was suggested that contact with them could make the children sick.

Whatever research plans or programs may be contemplated by Government Health authorities, at camp level it is difficult for a transient observer to form any other impression than that nobody really cares about doing anything positive to alleviate short or long term problems of Aboriginal health in this area.

Hamilton (1971) made several positive recommendations which she felt from her experience of living with the people would at least directionally help to alleviate some of the health problems. In 1975 it is hard to see any progress in the key areas she highlighted such as making available more nutritional and acceptable foods like high protein white flour, such as a training program for medical staff working with Aboriginals in the social and cultural practices of the people particularly as they affect health matters or any attempt to meld the European and traditional health practices into some worthwhile form by involving the *wati* doctors in the prevention and cure of European diseases. The only positive step has been the result of the people's own initiative in moving away from settlements to smaller decentralised camps where some bush foods help the nutritional levels and ability to move camp more readily to new ground helps to solve hygiene problems in the traditional manner.

5.10 SACRED SITES

An aspect of Pitjantjatjara religion very relevant to the decentralisation initiative is the strength of the relationship of the men to their sacred sites. In the following section an attempt is made to assess this at least superficially from the observed emotions and behaviour of Pitjantjatjara men on visits to these sites.

Whilst Pipalyatjara itself does not appear to have great religious significance the surrounding area is dotted with important sites, the most important of which were visited with the Pipalyatjara men. No attempt will be made to recount the mythology of each site which as yet is poorly comprehended, but certain impressions were gained again and again from observing the behaviour of the men at their sacred sites.

The over-riding impression was that whatever erosion of economic or social values may have occurred through European contact the spiritual significance of religious sites remains a strong and unshakeable part of the men's philosophy. It is not so much that the men's behaviour at sacred sites exhibits the awe and hushed reverence that one would expect to see shown by Christians at a sacred shrine, but almost the reverse. In my view the strength of the man/site tie is more strongly demonstrated by the "matter of factness" of the man's attitude. Certain ordained ritual must be carried out when first approaching the site. For example, at one site the men split into two groups and ran in a wide semi-circle to meet at the site. At all sites the first action of all the men was to clean the site of grass or sand which was obscuring the sacred rocks and then each man in turn would slowly press his body against each rock to receive into themselves some of the ancestral potency. However, once this ritual was carried out the men would sit around by the rocks or even on them, discussing some of the finer points of the mythology of the site or explaining details to younger men. Voices may be raised in disagreement over a detail, a man may cry as he thinks of sad things that happened to an ancestral hero, or a relative if he is in his presence, yet others may be laughing and joking about an ancestral feat. The whole atmosphere was relaxed. The impression gained on every occasion was that there was nothing for the people to question or prove, it was all matters of fact there, both visibly (for everyone to see) and in the narratives.

The sites fell into two broad classes. The first were natural features created by ancestral heroes during their wanderings in the Dreaming, such as the rockholes created by the *malu kutjara* when they rested or natural features which are the particular ancestral heroes in their final resting place. The second were man-made rock arrangements, some simple, some comprising hundreds of stones arranged in a pattern which were the people's direct ancestors like old *Kata* who is the grandfather *(tjamu)* of many of the Pipalyatjara men. In both cases the sites are very sacred *(milmilpa)* and forbidden to all but fully initiated men. This prohibition carries over to Europeans. On one occasion we had a young European man with us who was an adult in our society but because he was not married with children he was not a *"wati pulka"* and was not allowed to visit the sites even though he was held in high regard by the people.

The Pipalyatjara men, particularly the "owners" of particular sites, have a strong sense of guardianship over the sites and are determined not to allow them to be desecrated by visits of unaccompanied Europeans. It is important in the maintenance of the people's religion which is entwined into the whole fabric of their society that the secrecy and sanctity of these sites be respected. It is debatable in my view whether the present activity of mapping and recording these sites with the laudable objective of declaring them prohibited areas will decrease or increase the possibility of violation. There are many rock painting sites in other parts of the continent which are in need of urgent conservation measures as well as legal or physical protection against vandalism. However, these natural rocks and stone arrangements will not deteriorate and although their locations are of course well known to the people themselves they are not readily visible or accessible to outsiders. My view simply is that until the Pitjantjatjara have some legal ownership of their land and ability to enforce access restriction the less European attention of any sort directed towards their sites the more secure they will be. Likewise the erection of signs (see plate 5.10:1) is more likely to draw attention to a site than deter intruders.

There can be no doubt in the mind of anyone who has spent even the briefest time with the people that these sites are the sacred shrines of a real and living religion and as such both the morality and law of our society demand their sanctity against desecration in the name of either science or economic progress.

Plate 5.10:1 Sacred site warning sign erected near a ritual site in the Tomkinson Ranges.

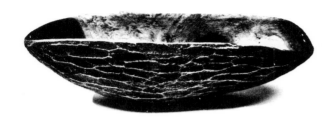

6

THE CONTEMPORARY CRAFTS
OF THE PITJANTJATJARA

Plate 6.1:3 Western Desert man working with a stone chisel
mounted on a spear-thrower. The Western Desert
spear-thrower was a multi-purpose artifact, besides
being an efficient spear-thrower it was used as a
receptacle, fire-making saw and a wood working tool.
Western Desert, 1933.

THE CONTEMPORARY CRAFTS
OF THE PITJANTJATJARA

Plate 6.1:1   Traditional Pitjantjatjara leaf-shaped spear throwers.

Plate 6.1:2   An older Pitjantjatjara spear thrower smeared with the blood of kangaroos killed from its use.

6.1   SPEAR   THROWER *(Miru)* — Plate 6.1:1

Description and Uses

Whilst made primarily for sale, many of the older men make and retain a spear thrower and three or four spears *(kulata)* by their *wiltja* as their personal weapons although they are very seldom used now as such. The spear thrower described above (see plate 6.1:2) is a typical personal one which was used to hunt kangaroos and, as was the custom, was smeared with the blood of animals speared.

Made from the trunk of a mulga tree *(Acacia aneura)* the blade is 87 cm long, 8.6 cm wide at the widest point and quite concave in shape with the depth of concavity being 2.5 cm. The weapon blade is deliberately made thin (approximately 2 mm) and flexible which adds a whipping action to the launching of the spear. The total weight of this specimen is only 450 g.

The spear peg *(mukulpa)* is a sharpened piece of hardwood (usually from a *Eucalypt*) 4 cm long by 0.6 cm diameter which is lashed to the end of the blade at an angle of approximately 20° by means of kangaroo sinew. On the distal end of the spear thrower a stone adzing flake *(kanti)* is set using spinifex resin *(kiti)*. In the weapon described the semi-discoidal flake of chert measured 3 cm by 2.5 cm showed no evidence of secondary working and was set in a piece of gum 6 cm × 5 cm × 3 cm with 1 cm protruding. The back of the spear thrower blade has a flat convex shape about its longitudinal axis with a depth of convexity of 1.5 cm. A random sample of six Pitjantjatjara spear throwers made during the last four years was examined and whilst there were variations in dimensions of up to 10% above and below those quoted above, all specimens exhibited a close conformity of design and shape.

Well chronicled and confirmed by older Pitjantjatjara informants the spear thrower had multiple uses. It was also used as a woodworking adze (plate 6.1:3), a receptacle mainly for blood and ochre during ceremonies and as a fire making saw. It is a most elegant practical example of Western Desert craftsmanship.

Historical Information

From reports of the first travellers who visited the Western Desert there is no doubt that the spear thrower was an item of the traditional meagre tool kit of the Pitjantjatjara. In 1891 Helms (1896:269-270) described spear throwers from the Everard and Blythe Ranges with the same shape and characteristics as the present day but about 20 cm shorter. In 1903 Basedow (1904:25) described and sketched spear throwers from the Musgrave Ranges which again appear similar except that an additional blob of gum is shown a few centimetres from the adze holding gum evidently to give the thrower a better grip. The similarity in design can be noticed in plate 2:2 which is a photograph taken by Dr. Hackett in the Musgrave Ranges in 1933. In 1940 Mountford (1941: 312-316) recorded and photographed the manufacture of a spear thrower by people from the Mann Ranges and in 1963 Thomson (1964:400-422) recorded two Pitjantjatjara men who had had virtually no European contact making a spear thrower. All of the spear throwers described above were made with stone tools and they show evident similarity to the present steel tool product and the lack of change over this 80 year period. In the only example where some dimensions are given Thomson's spear thrower is only 2 cm longer (89 cm .) and has exactly the same longitudinal convexity (1.5 cm) as the present day specimens described previously. Both Tindale and Thomson record also that the finished weapon is smeared with red ochre as the only decoration.

Davidson (1936:445-483) in his study of the spear thrower in Australia gives evidence to show that this particular type of Central Australian spear thrower was found from Barrow Creek, N.T. to northern South Australia and across to eastern Western Australia, which he suggests is a local variation of the broad leaf-like spear throwers which were found from western Queensland to the far west coast and from the Kimberley district to the southern coast. McCarthy's (1940:248) contention that this variation with its multi-use function (spear thrower, adzing tool, receptacle and fire saw) was developed as a substitute to avoid the need to carry other implements would appear most logical. The most pertinent local invention was the traits which improved its efficiency in its primary use as a spear thrower, namely its lightness, flexibility and longitudinal convexity. This is not found in any other type of spear thrower and could have developed because of the generally open terrain and dependance on large and possibly scarce game (kangaroo and emu) requiring the fastest possible spear launching velocity for accuracy and distance. Obviously it was adequate to enable the men to stalk and kill these animals but quantification or range is liable to exaggeration. Travelling through the area in 1932 a reliable observer, Finlayson (1935:82) stated that the accuracy of spear and spear thrower was as good or better than an average shot with a rifle up to 60 yds. More precise are the observations of Gill (1970:122) who organised a competition in spear throwing by a group of nomadic Pitjantjatjara in the Peterman Ranges in 1931. The longest throw was 50 cm and a hit and near misses were recorded in a 40 cm by 15 cm target at 33 m.

Method of Manufacture

The method of manufacture of a Western Desert spear thrower is descried by Mountford (1941:312-316) and in considerable

detail by Thomson (1964:412-416). In both cases stone tools were used. Plates 6.1:4 to 6.1:14 show the main stages of manufacture of a spear thrower by Jacky Mirankura at Pipalyatjara in February 1975 and the only additional comments which will be made are to note any variations in method caused by the change from stone tools to steel tools for, as mentioned earlier, the end product by both methods appears identical.

The use of steel axes and tomahawks in place of stone hand axes and choppers has widened the range of suitable mulga trees and simplified the procedure of removing the initial flitch of timber. In the procedures recorded by both Tindale and Thomson, a straight-grained mulga about 8" in diameter at the base was selected and notches cut at the top (Tindale) or right around the shape of flitch (Thomson) before it was removed using timber wedges. The removed flitch after stripping the bark had the required curvature and subsequent working and removal of heartwood was simplified.

As shown in plates 6.1:4 and 6.1:5 a larger diameter tree was used and by cutting rough notches top and bottom and by use of tomahawks as wedges a larger unshaped flitch could be quite quickly removed. Most of the subsequent shaping is expertly performed using only a tomahawk (plates 6.1:6 and 6.1:7). This operation replaced the careful and laborious removal of the heartwood using stone hand choppers transversely across the grain to remove small chips. Whilst Thomson records this process took several days, with the use of a tomahawk initial shaping can be completed in four or five hours.

Final smoothing and shaping was performed using an adaptation of the traditional adzing tool made by welding a chisel blade to a piece of pipe (see plates 6.1:8 and 6.11:2) but the process of planing and scraping by resting the end of the spear thrower against the heel and using a vertical motion with the tool at an angle of approximately 30° is identical with the method described by Tindale.
The process of fitting the hardwood spear peg, chewing a length of kangaroo sinew to soften it then using this as a lashing is identical with the traditional method (see plates 6.1:9-11).

Likewise the process of softening a piece of spinifex gum over the fire, moulding it around the spear thrower distal end and fitting the adzing flake (plates 6.1:12-14) is identical with the traditional method described by Tindale and Thomson. The method of making the spinifex gum is described later in this report.

Conclusion

The Pitjantjatjara spear thrower has been discussed at some length because it is perhaps the best example of the retention of a method of manufacture and form of a traditional item of material culture. This may be due in part to the fact that some of the people still use a spear thrower, albeit infrequently, it still used ceremonially, but more importantly there has been no pressure by Europeans to upset the people's mental template of a traditional spear thrower; whilst the financial return in European terms is not high (about $8 for about ten hours work) the making of spear throwers is an activity enjoyed by the craftsman and as recorded by Thomson it becomes a socially cohesive occasion with several men often sitting around discussing and offering advice to the craftsmen as the work proceeds (plate 6.1:7).

Plates 6.1:4-14 This series of photographs show the techniques used by Jackie Mirankura of the Western Pitjantjatjara to make a spearthrower.

Plate 6.1:4 V-shaped cuts are made in a suitable mulga tree at the top and bottom of the selected flitch of timber. A tomahawk is inserted as a side wedge.

Plate 6.1:5 The flitch of timber is removed.

Plate 6.1:6 A tomahawk is used for initial shaping. In traditional times a stone-axe was used for this purpose.

41

Plate 6.1:7 The spear thrower quickly takes shape in the hands of an expert craftsman.

Plate 6.1:8 Final shaping is completed using an adzing tool.

Plate 6.1:9 Kangaroo sinew is used to bind the spear peg to the blade. It is softened by chewing.

Plate 6.1:10 The hardwood peg is securely bound to the blade with the softened kangaroo sinew.

Plate 6.1:11   The sinew is pulled tight and bitten off.

Plate 6.1:12   A ball of spinifex gum is softened over the fire and moulded around the spear thrower handle.

Plate 6.1:13   A quartz cutting flake is pushed into the softened gum.

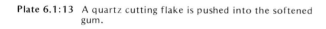

Plate 6.1:14   The gum is moulded around the stone flake with the cutting edge set at right angles to the longitudinal axis of the spear thrower. The gum becomes hard when it has cooled.

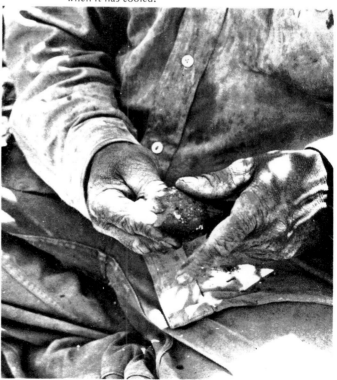

6.2 HUNTING SPEAR *(Kulata)* — Plate 6.2:1

Description and Uses

The material used is the long thin branches of the Tecoma bush *(Pandorea doratoxylon)* which is comparatively rare in the area. The spears described were made from Tecoma bushes growing in rocky crevices of Mt Caroline, 50 km south-west of Amata (plate 6.2:2). I did not see or hear of the use of the branches of the Witchetty Bush (Acacia kempeana) mentioned by Cleland (1966:120) or the use of the roots of dwarf Acacias mentioned by Thomson (1964:421) and Gould (1969:86) for the people further west.

The typical currently manufactured spear illustrated in plate 6.2:1 has the following characteristics. It is made in three sections which are lashed together with kangaroo or emu sinew. The main shaft is 2.2 m long tapering from a diameter of 1.2 cm at the tail to 1.8 cm at the head. The throwing extension *(palka)* is 32 cm long 1.4 cm diameter and is also made from Tecoma. The end is slightly whittled down and a shallow recess formed to fit the end of the spear thrower peg. The spear head *(wata)* is made from mulga *(Acacia aneura)* is 22 cm long 2 cm wide at the base widening out to 3 cm before coming back to a sharp point. The head 0.8 cm thick whilst 10 cm from the point a hardwood barb 4 cm by 0.5 cm diameter is lashed with sinew at an angle of approximately 20° to the spear head. The total length 2.7 m (approx. 9 ft) and the total weight 370 g. The centre of gravity of the spear is 1.2 m from the point.

This type of spear has been designed for maximum efficiency and utility as a projectile for hunting large game. The three piece construction simplified maintenance. The hardwood mulga wood point can be readily sharpened or replaced whilst the short section which fits into the spear thrower has evidently proved to be the section most subject to damage or stress in storage or throwing. Likewise the detachable barb can be readily replaced.

Historical Information

The observations of the first white men to visit the Musgrave, Mann, Tomkinson Range area indicates that this type of spear was part of the Pitjantjatjara men's tool kit pre-contact. In 1903 Basedow (1904:25) describes the hunting and fighting spear of the Pitjantjatjara in this area as almost identical to the current specimen described above. He gives the name of the spear as *"oritchanna"* which is more correctly the Pitjantjatjara name for the Tecoma bush from which it is made *"urtjanpa"*.

Davidson (1934:144) in a survey of Australian spear traits indicates that this type of composite spear with a detachable barb extended through central Australia into South Australia. Davidson further suggests that this type of spear developed in central Australia but as McCarthy (1940:269) points out this is open to doubt as there were composite three piece spears in Queensland and on the Sepik River in New Guinea.

Spencer and Gillen (1855:577) describe spears identical in design and very similar in dimensions used by the Urubunna, Ilpirra, Luritcha and Arunta tribes who lived in central Australia to the north-east of the Pitjantjatjara.

Plate 6.2:1 The traditional Pitjantjatjara hunting spear, *kulata*. The top two illustrations show the flat hardwood spear-head and barb lashed to the spear shaft and the bottom illustration shows the short tail section likewise lashed to the shaft with kangaroo sinew.

Method of Manufacture

The first stage is to cut the long flexible branches from the Tecoma bush and remove the leaves and twigs. Whilst the stems are green and flexible they are carefully heated by passing over a small fire so the shafts can be straightened, often wedging them in the for of a tree support. The shafts are carefully reheated and turned over the fire as necessary so that straightening can continue until completed. The shaft is also gripped in the teeth using them as a vice to straighten minor variations with pressure from both hands.

The straight shaft is then planed down using a knife or rasp until a smooth straight shaft approximately 2 m to 2.5 m long and tapering from a little over 1 cm at one end to up to 2 cm at the other is achieved. The throwing end section is made in a similar fashion into a length of Tecoma 32 to 40 cm in length and about 1.5 cm in diameter. The circular spear thrower peg recess is cut with a knife and the end which will join the main shaft is cut off diagonally at an angle of about 20° to the axis of the spear. The end of the main shaft is cut off at the same angle and a small amount of spinifex gum placed between the two parts as an adhesive.

This is then tightly bound together with kangaroo or emu sinew which has been softened by chewing as described in the section on the spear thrower. The contraction of the sinew on drying combined with the setting of the gum produce a joint which is as strong as the shaft itself. The spear head whose dimensions were given earlier is simply fashioned out of a piece of mulga using a knife and chisel adze and fastened to the main shaft in the same manner as the throwing end section. The mulga or other hard wood barb is shaped with a knife or chisel adze so that one end sits flat on the spear blade and thus can be securely lashed with sinew around the blade itself (see plate 6.2:1).

Conclusions

As with the spear thrower whilst the tools of manufacture have changed from stone to steel much of the technology and as far as can be determined the complete form has remained unchanged since European contact. Whilst seldom if ever used for hunting now *kulatas* are still very much a part of some of the older men's possessions as a status symbol, for settling disputes and for ceremonial purposes.

6.3 WOODEN CONTAINERS *(Wira, Kanilypa, Piti).*

Plate 6.3:3 Hardwood bowl called a *wira* made at Pipalyatjara in 1973. Traditionally they were used as digging tools to open the burrows of lizards and small marsupials.

Description and Uses

The Pitjantjatjara women today make a number of different sizes and shapes of wooden bowls to which Europeans apply the general term *Coolamon*. The bowls are made entirely by women as artifacts for sale as their use for carrying, winnowing and digging has been almost completely superseded by either European type containers or adaptations of wooden bowls made from steel (see plate 6.3:13).

Many of the bowls still made are replicas of traditional bowls which the women have categorised as follows:—

- *Piti* — A large bowl which is eccentrically carved in longitudinal section as well as its transverse convexity and ranges in size from about 45 cm by 25 cm wide up to about 80 cm long by 30 cm wide. It was used as a receptacle carried on the women's head mainly for water. Plates 6.3:1 and 2:1 from photographs taken by Dr. Hackett in the Musgrave Ranges in 1933 show traditional *pitis* whilst the photograph on page 1 indicates a modern example. The material used may be branches of mulga *(Acacia aneura)* blood wood *(Eucalyptus corymbosa)* quondong *(Santalum acuminatum)* or the roots of the river red gum *(Eucalyptus camaldulensis).*

The example shown in the photograph on page 1 has the following dimensions. Length 70 cm breadth 21 cm depth at deepest part 19 cm and approximate thickness 5 mm and weighs 2.2 kg.

- *Kanilypa* — A smaller bowl which is flatter in longitudinal section with a straight top and varies in size, from about 40 cm long by 12 cm wide to almost 60 cm long by 30 cm wide. The current example shown in plate (6.3:2) is 48 cm long by 14 cm wide and 8 cm deep. The average thickness is about 4 mm and the weight 600 g. It was used mainly as a winnowing and separating dish for edible grass seeds and as a receptacle for collecting fruits and berries. It is made from the same materials as the *Piti.*

- *Wira* — This is a smaller bowl again which was basically a digging tool. It is flat on the top and generally more convex in longitudinal section than the *kanilypa* (see plate 6.3:3). It varies in size from about 20 cm long by 8 cm wide to about 35 cm long by 15 cm wide. The current example pictured is 28 cm long by 9 cm wide and 6 cm deep. It has an average thickness of about 3 mm and weighs 150 g. A smaller version of the *wira* called a *kimpiri* is made for use by children.

Plate 6.3:2 Wooden bowls of many different shapes and sizes are made by the women for a range of uses. This particular type is a *kanilypa* used for winnowing seeds and carrying berries and fruits.

All the above bowls have been made to the same design by the Pitjantjatjara women over the last few years and are still being made as replicas of the bowls which they assert were made *iriti* (long ago). They are all rubbed with red ochre when completed and the outside is finished with a ridged and crenulated effect which reproduces evidently the marks left when the bowls were adzed with the semidiscoidal mounted stone tools. The inside surface is now smoothed but it is likely that the same tools would have been used for the inside surface and traditionally this could have exhibited the same pattern.

In addition to the traditional type bowls the women now add what is assumed for lack of any early contact evidence to be a recent innovation of decorating the backs of bowls with incised designs. These designs are beautifully and artistically created as the craftswomens interpretation of the stories and myths told to them in childhood. See plates 6.3:4 and 6.3:5.

Whilst the practice of burning rough designs on artifacts has been known for some years it was not until 1971 that the women were encouraged to use their innate artistic skill to record myths and stories using known symbolism. Full credit for this encouragement which was eagerly and happily taken up by the Amata women is due to Mr. David Abrams who was appointed crafts officer at Amata in 1970. Mr Abrams collected and translated many of the stories and with full support from the Superintendent at the time Mr David Hope was responsible for the revival of a traditional craft in a new form which had what I would postulate to be a socially cohesive affect of maintaining interest and awareness of traditional stories and myths.

Mr Abrams translated the following comments about this by one of the craftswomen Nelly Paterson which is reproduced below:

"Our grandmothers are always talking. Always speaking, sitting around, telling stories, drawing in the sand. And we listen to stories they are telling. The women, having spoken and spoken, always tell stories. And the children, listening, say: 'Yes. Yes. Go on.' And the grandmothers always tell stories; they are always telling stories. "Did you understand that story?" And they say: 'I heard it. Yes. I understand it". And talking, drawing in the sand they say: ' . . . and the Snake woman was laying down over there. For three days she travelled away from the others, by herself, making camp with her children . . ."

And grandmother tells her stories. And little grandfather also. Talking, talking and talking. And the children and us say "Yes. Yes grandmother".

And it is said in the olden times, beating the sand with a stick, they were telling stories. And now, thinking of these stories, we tell them and draw them. These stories are caused to rise in our work. And we work truly hard making these stories rise by drawing.

From these stories we draw a lot and from this we are given quite a lot of money. And they are being sent away to Adelaide, Melbourne, Sydney and Canberra. To all different places they are being sent. One wood only, from Amata, to many places. And it becoming wide.

Plate 6.3:1 Wooden bowls were the only utensils of the Pitjantjatjara women. Woman with her child carrying water back to camp in a *piti*. Musgrave Ranges, 1933.

Having learnt the stories from our grandmothers we draw them on the *coolamons*. From these stories that grandfather and grandmother have taught us, we remember and draw them. The ones we have learnt to tell from our grandfather and grandmother."

47

Plate 6.3:4 Beautifully incised carrying bowl *kanilypa* which illustrated the Pitjantjatjara story "Two Children". Length 60 cm width 20 cm.

Plate 6.3:5 Further example of the artistic interpretative designs of the Pitjantjatjara women. This design tells the story "The Sname Woman". Length 40 cm width 20 cm.

"TWO CHILDREN"

And they, having sat and sat one night, saw some lightning shining on everything. A lot of lightning. Happily, they went closer to the lightning and went to sleep. And early the next morning they got up and hurried along. And they carefully approached and saw something almost bent over them. A snake. And, running there, they speared it in the head.
And having speared it, they were dragging it around. It was half dead. They coiled it around their heads. And it started moving there and almost tied them up, wrapping itself around them. And the two boys, becoming frightened, threw it down. At Iyarka². They threw it down at Iyarka.
And then they got up and tried to stand it up and said: "It's not dead! It's still alive! It moved!"
And having got up, they were standing it up and singing. But they could not make it stand up, so they coiled it around their heads.
And it died completely. And they coiled it up. Coiling it, they stood it up.

"SNAKE WOMAN"

Now I am going to tell you a Pitjantjatjara story from our dreaming. When I was a child I heard this story about KUNIYA, a carpet snake we eat, that lives in the sandhill country.
Some women were going to make a new camp closeby. And one woman, carrying her children on her back, could not keep up with the rest. A Snake-woman. And she was singing as she carried her children, the others having left her behind. And it is said that she was singing:
"Could somebody help me,
By carrying my children for me.
Could somebody help me,
By carrying my children for me . . ."
And each day she camped apart from the others, not being able to catch them up, not going as far as they – lying down half way. For three days she travelled before she joined them.
And having walked and walked and stayed apart for three days she arrived at the others' camp – because they had stopped. And when they came together they camped.
And that woman always carried her children on her back. Like big eggs. KUNIYA still carry their children as eggs.
We tell this story amongst ourselves. And having heard this story all the women know how to make the designs on the coolamons. They have heard about this snake – this meat of ours.

Narrated by Lanky. Translated by A. Minuntjukur and L. Abrams. Copyright vested in the Amata Society.

Narrated by Charlie Ilyatjari. Translated by A. Minuntjukur and L. Abrams. Copyright vested in the Amata Society.

Historical information

All early travellers to the area record a wooden bowl carried on the women's head for transporting food and water as an invariable part of the peoples tool kit. The evidence is not however, completely conclusive that hardwood bowls of the types and with the uses mentioned previously were the only wooden receptacles used by the Pitjantjatjara in pre-contact times. For the people in the Blythe Range south of the Tomkinson Ranges, Helms in 1891 (Helms 1896:270) records that the people like the Everard Range people had a small wooden digging bowl less than one foot long called a *wera* and a large deep oblong water bowl made of solid wood and gouged out *(mika).*

However, Basedow in 1903 (Basedow 1904: 25-26) reports the same two types of bowls but says they were invariably made of soft wood usually the bark of eucalypts.

The later evidence is more conclusive. The photographs (plates 6.3:1 and 2:1) taken by Dr. Hackett in 1933 previously referred to conform to the present day *piti.* Love (1942: 215-217) records the names and uses of the three types of bowls *(piti, kanilypa, wira)* in identical terms to those described with the material used being the trunk of the white stemmed gum *(Eucalyptus rostrata).*

It would appear likely that these hardwood bowls of similar designs were made and used in pre-contact times but it is possible that they were supplemented with softwood bark containers.

Method of Manufacture

As mentioned previously the materials used at present are the branches of mulga, bloodwood and quondong or the roots of a eucalypt. Plates (6.3:6-11) show the main stages in manufacturing a *kanilypa* from the roots of a river red gum *(Eucalyptus camaldulensis)* but the method is essentially the same for the different types of source materials.

Love (1942:215-217) recorded the manufacture of *kanilypa* using stone tools at Ernabella in 1942 and although they had been introduced to steel tools a few years previously they tried well remembered techniques so it is relevant to note the differences in method now evident with steel tools. With the stone tooled dish the trunk of a white stemmed gum *(Eucalyptus rostrata)* which was hollow was selected and virtually the finished outline of the *kanilypa* was chopped from the trunk.

As mentioned with reference to the changes in manufacture of the spear thrower the introduction of the steel axe particularly has widened the range of available timber and changed the initial stages of manufacture quite markedly. As shown in plates 6.3 : 5-6, the whole root stem (or tree limb) of a sound tree is cut into the required length and the bowl largely shaped from a solid block of wood using an axe and tomahawk (plates 6.3:7-8).

The final smoothing and finishing previously performed with the stone adzing tool *(kantitjara)* is now performed with a piece of fencing wire about 30 cms long bent over into a loop at both ends. One end serves as a handle whilst the other end is heated in the coals of a fire so that a curved impression can be burnt into the bowl to form the design (see plate 6.3:12).

Another process mentioned by Love was to heat the bowl when adzing was completed in the ashes of a fire and place transverse sticks as props to stop the top thin edges curling inwards. This is now seldom necessary as the curling is minimised by construction from a solid block of wood. In the construction of large eccentric *pitis* a bough or root is selected at a point where it has a natural bend so that the sharply curved shape (see plate 6.3:1) can be more easily obtained.

Conclusions

As the wooden bowls are no longer used for their original purpose in the women's daily life the tendency for change and adaptation has been more pronounced. The adaptation of using burnt designs has retained some traditionality by the depiction through them of stories and myths and there has wisely been no pressure on the people to prostitute this adaptation into European type souvenirs. Munn (1965:21) records how the Pitjantjatjara women at Areyonga used pieces of wire or stick to graphically represent in the sand parts of a story they were telling. This adaptation at Amata has enabled them to extend this type of activity. However, just as importantly my observations of the Pitjantjatjara craftsmen doing this work from 1971 indicated to me that it was a force in developing the women's dignity and sense of achievement for which settlement life gave few opportunities.

The artistic ability of the women in creating and burning these designs depicting old stories and myths is well illustrated in plates 6.3:4 and 6.3:5 of two incised bowls and the stories they represent.

Plate 6.3:12   Pieces of wire heated in the fire are used to incise traditional "story" designs on to carrying bowls.

6.3:13   Hub caps are sometimes adapted for use as *wiras.*

Plates 6.3:6–11 Stages in the manufacture of a carrying bowl *Kanilypa* from the roots of a River Red Gum, Tomkinson Ranges.

Plate 6.3:6 Digging out a suitable root to be fashioned into a carrying bowl.

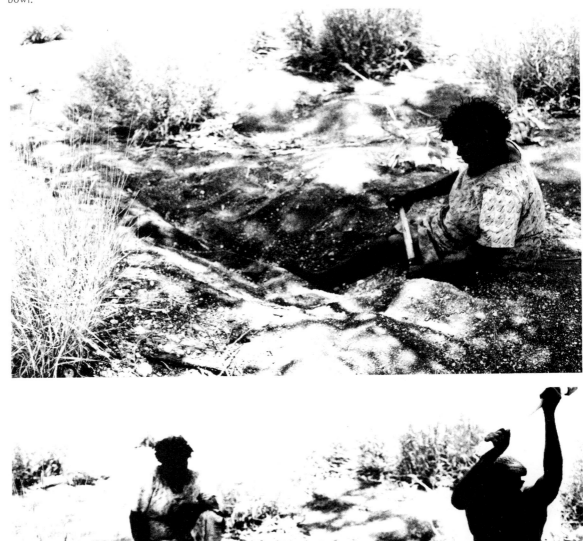

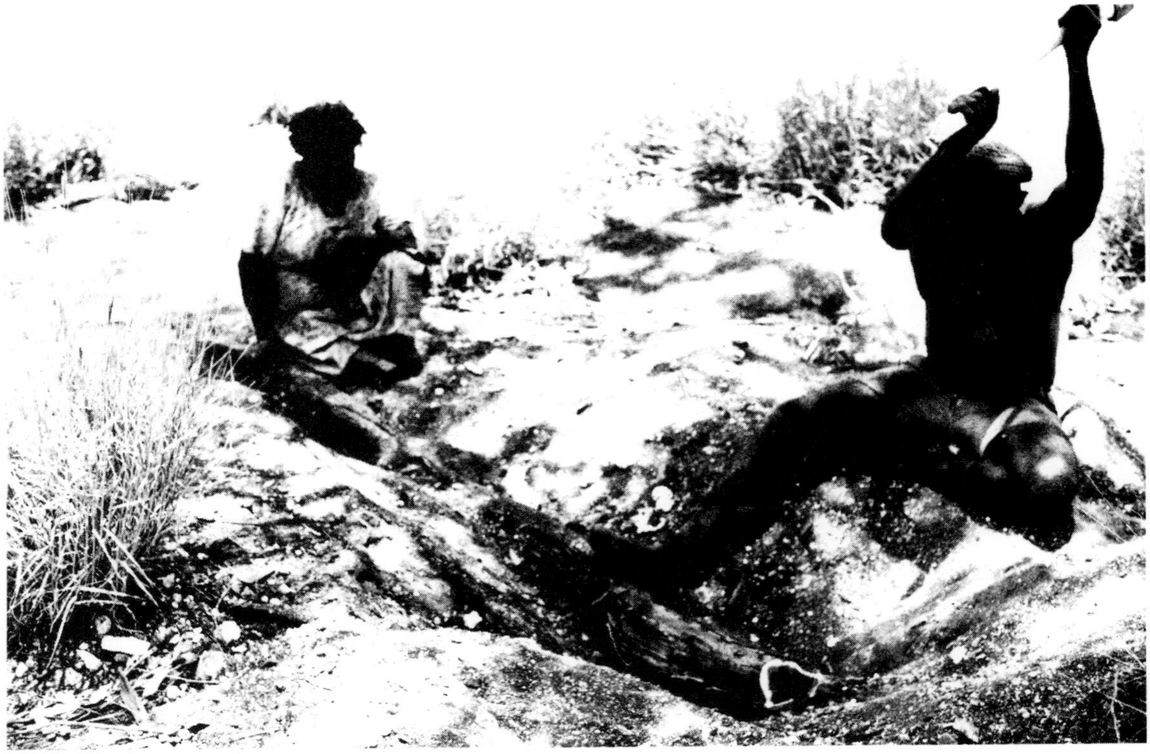

Plate 6.3:7 Cutting the hard-wood root into the appropriate lengths for the bowls.

Plate 6.3:8 Rough shaping with a steel axe.

Plate 6.3:9 Further shaping. It takes a skilled craftsman about an hour to rough out the shape.

Plate 6.3:10 The bowl is finally shaped with very skilful use of a tomahawk.

Plate 6.3:11 A wood rasp or pieces of broken glass are used for the final smoothing and finishing.

6.4 WOMEN'S DIGGING STICK *(Wana)*

Description

Plate 6.4:1 shows a current example of a digging stick made by Pitjantjatjara women. The example illustrated is typical and is 80 cm by 4.5 cm in diameter and weighs 1.2 kg. It has a sharpened and fire hardened point. The material used is mulga wood. These are made mainly for sale although occasionally may be used for digging up edible tubers. For digging out rabbits and lizards it has been superseded by the short handled shovel and crowbar.

Historical Information

There seems to be no doubt that a digging stick called a *wana* was part of the precontact tool kit of the Pitjantjatjara. Whether it was in the same form as described above is not clear although White (1915:728) describes "a thick mulga stick called *wanna* from 2 ft. (61 cm) to 3 ft. (91 cm) long sharpened at one end hardened by fire . . . used principally for digging out food" carried by the Everard and Musgrave Range women in 1914. Helms (1895:270) refers to a digging stick called a *wanna* used in the Everard and Blyth Ranges in 1891 whilst Basedow (1904:26) refers to a large digging stick called a *wanna* up to 180 cm in length which is used by both males and females but generally the latter.

Spencer and Gillen (1899:26) describes for tribes to the north of the Pitjantjatjara how the short digging stick is used as a one handed pick held near the blade for loosening soil whilst the other hand or a small *pitchi* (the Pitjantjatjara *wira*) is used to clear it away.

Method of Manufacture

The *wana* is simply and readily made from a suitable mulga branch by scraping and planing using metal adzing tools, rasps and knives.

Conclusion

It is of interest to note that without any outside suggestions or market pressure (very few of these items are in fact bought) that the *wanas* turn out almost identical in dimensions and shape which one could postulate confirms some antiquity for the existence of a precise mental template but this is conjectural.

Plate 6.4:1   The Pitjantjatjara women's digging stick *wana.*

6.5   SPUN HAIR AND FUR ARTICLES

Description and Method of Manufacture

The Pitjantjatjara women spin human hair and animal fur to make a number of traditional items of adornment and use as well as spinning wool both for sale as spun wool and for themselves to make crocheted berets and woven belts and other articles.

The spinning is done using a simple spinning frame (see plate 6.5:1) made from twigs of the wild Tecoma bush. It consists of a pair of cross arms *(kuntil)* about 0.5 cm in diameter and about 20 cm long which are split for a few centimetres in the centre and placed at right angles to each other through the shaft *(inti)* which is about 60 to 70 cm long and usually a little greater in diameter than the cross pieces which are placed about 25 cm from one end.

To spin about 15 cm of thread is hand spun and fixed to the junction of the cross arms while the free end is held. The inti is then rotated on the spinner's thigh so that the thread is twisted. Whilst the thread is held to prevent its untwisting teased hair or wool is pressed into the free end. The twisted threads is then released and as it unravels it picks up the added length of hair or wool causing it to be twisted in the unravelling process. The spinner then retwists the new length overtwisting it until the permanency of the twist is ensured then winds the excess length onto the cross arms.

The process continues until a ball of thread has been spun onto the frame. The frame is dismantled by pulling out first the shaft then the cross arms. The two ends of the ball of thread are joined and wound double into a ball. The double thread is then spun in the reverse direction to the original twist to produce a tight two-ply thread.

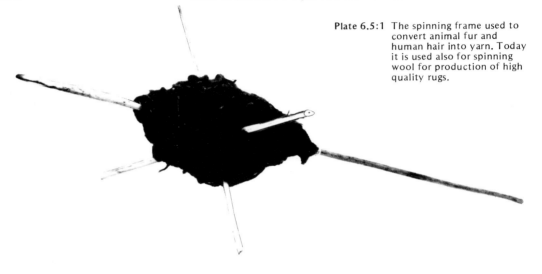

Plate 6.5:1 The spinning frame used to convert animal fur and human hair into yarn. Today it is used also for spinning wool for production of high quality rugs.

Some of the items then made with the fur or hair thread are as follows:

Manguri — plate 6.5:4.

This is the traditional head ring on which the *piti* or *kanilypa* was placed for carrying. It is made by twisting a piece of bark into a circular shape and winding spun fur or hair around it until a soft circular pad approximately 7 cm inside diameter and 15 cm outside diameter is built up. It is now seldom used for this purpose as although the women use their heads for carrying objects there are now European containers for water or food of such diverse shapes and sizes that a piece of rag folded to suit the container being carried is used.

Plate 6.5:4 The traditional women's head-pad *manguri* enabled the women to carry wooden bowls *piti* on their heads.

Plate 6.5:5 Traditional penis ornament *maranga* made from spun human hair and animal fur.

Maranga — plate 6.5:5.

This is the traditional men's penis ornament which is made from spun hair or fur twisted and knotted at the centre into a roughly semi-circular shape. The specimen pictured had a radius of approximately 8.5 cm .

Plate 6.5:6 Traditional men's hair belt *nanpa* made from spun human hair and animal fur.

Nanpa — plate 6.5:6

This is a hair belt made from spun hair twisted double to make a thicker and stronger thread. The specimen pictured has 28 strands each 60 cm long. I have not seen it worn presently although it could possibly be used on ritual occasions by the men.

Plate 6.5:7 Traditional women's hair skirt *mawulyari* made from spun human hair and animal fur.

Mawulyari — plate 6.5:7

A women's hair skirt. The specimen pictured consists of 44 lengths of double twisted hair thread each 25 cm long knotted over a double twisted thread belt. It is no longer used except perhaps ceremonially.

55

Adapted Craft

Many of the younger women are very keen to develop their skills in weaving and crocheting wool combined with work in leather to make a range of useful items. Two of the items are crocheted bags (plate 6.5:8) and leather and crocheted wool berets (plate 6.5:9). These latter are purchased and worn by people themselves and as the women work together happily on this work it may in time be extended to provide more of the clothing needs of the people.

Historical Information

The spinning of fur and hair using the method described was a traditional and according to Hilliard (1968:101) a unique Australian Aboriginal skill. Encountering a nomadic group in the Peterman Ranges in 1931 Gill (1970:128) reported "yet surprisingly I saw a woman spinning. She was using a hand operated spindle — a primitive thing made from wood slivers so delicate that they looked like strips of split bamboo. The twine she spun was from fur and human hair."

Hilliard (1968:171) records that the spinning of wool was introduced to the Pitjantjatjara at Ernabella about 1948.

Reference to other woven articles of adornment by early visitors to the area is not specific with the exception of hair belts which were used to carry small articles although Spencer and Gillen (1899:572) record the use of a similar though smaller fan shaped pubic tassel and a similar string skirt being used by the tribes further north.

Conclusion

The extraordinarily simple spinning frame and the complex technique of using it would both appear to be indigenous Aboriginal inventions. The Pitjantjatjara women are still extremely skilful and fast in its use and it is an activity which the older women like doing particularly. It has also led to the development of useful and high quality adapted crafts such as weaving of rugs, belts, scarves, etc. as well as crocheting and knitting, particularly amongst the Pitjantjatjara women at Ernabella.

Plate 6.5:9 Beret made from crocheted hand-spun wool and leather. These are widely worn by the Pitjantjatjara.

Given that the spinning technique was traditional it follows that at least some or all of the items utilising spun fur or human hair were also traditional but proof is lacking with regard to continuity of design. One woven article which from early accounts and photographs was traditional was the spun mens head band *(mitjilypa)* comprising several strands of spun fur or hair tightly wound across the forehead (plate 6.1:3). This may only be worn by initiated men who now use red wool for the same purpose.

Plate 6.5:8 Example of current Pitjantjatjara women's adapted craft. A crocheted bag made from wool hand-spun in the traditional way.

6.6 THE BOOMERANG *(Kali)*

Descriptions and Use

Three types of boomerangs are made all of a similar size and shape but differing with regard to absence of or type of design.

- Plain Boomerang (plate 6.6:1)
- Fluted Boomerang (plate 6.6:2)
- Incised Design Boomerang (plate 6.6:3)

The boomerangs are made from mulga wood are non-returning and would perhaps be more correctly termed throwing sticks. They are made entirely for sale. There are some variations in length and thickness but all those presently made show a similarity in the design characteristic of having a relatively flat curvature. In 20 current specimens selected at random length varied from 65 to 88 cm width from 5 to 8.5 cm and ratio of length to maximum rise from 9:1 to 14:1. Thickness was fairly standard at about 1 cm whilst weight varied from 350 g to 550 g.

Most specimens exhibit the characteristic shown in plates 6.6:1 and 6.6:3 of a slight reverse curvature on the top edge at the throwing end. In all specimens both edges were quite sharp whilst in cross-section either the back was flat with the front flatly curved or both sides were curved into a flat lenticular shape. The former cross-section was more general.

With the fluted boomerangs (see plate 6.6:2) it is normal for the flutes to be terminated about 12 cm from the throwing end and the same or a lesser distance from the other end. Depending on the width of the boomerang from 10 to 20 parallel flutes 2 to 3 mm wide and 1 mm deep are incised.

The incised design boomerangs feature the same type of fluting described above with the most frequent design being the one shown (see plate 6.6:3) where the boomerang is marked off into two sets of triangles. The direction of fluting in each of the top and bottom sets is maintained roughly parallel until the apex of the boomerang where both sets change direction to maintain roughly the same angle of incidence to the edge.

Plate 6.6:1 Hand crafted undecorated boomerang made from Mulga wood by Pitjantjatjara men.

Plate 6.6:2 Fluted boomerang used in traditional times over a large part of central Australia.

Plate 6.6:3 Intricate designs were often incised on the surface of boomerangs.

Plate 6.6:4 Stripping a suitable flitch of timber from a desert Mulga tree.

Plate 6.6:5 Initial shaping with a tomahawk. The craftsmen work quickly and precisely.

Method of Manufacture

The method of manufacture is very similar to that described for the spear thrower although the flitch of wood wedged from the mulga tree is shorter and flatter (plate 6.6:4). Most of the initial shaping is most skilfully done with a tomahawk only (plates 6.6:5-6) and finishing off with a rasp (plate 6.6:7). The fluting and incised designs are done with a narrow carpenter's chisel. Sand paper or a knife blade may be used to impart the smoothness and regularity which is a feature of the plain boomerangs.

Historical Information

The early observers are unanimous in their view that the people of this area neither made nor used boomerangs, see Helms (1896:270) Basedow (1904:24) White (1915:728) Gill in 1931 (1970:128). McCarthy (1961:343-349) from his study of the distribution of the types of boomerang in Australia delineates an area somewhat corresponding to the general Pitjantjatjara area as devoid of boomerangs of any type.

There are however some intriguing anomalies in this proposition. The old men insist that their fathers made boomerangs *iriti* (long ago). A few kilometres from Pipalyatjara are some rockholes called Ilitjata which is an important *Malu* (kangaroo) Dreaming site. The old men told me this story. Two of the large rockholes are the impressions made by the two mythical kangaroos *(malu kutjara)* when they rested there before going on to their final resting place at Puka Puka a few km away where the men showed me the two large semi-buried stones which are the *malu kutjara.* On the flat rock shelf beside a rockhole at Ilitjata the faint engravings of four boomerangs can be seen, two left handed, two right handed and also a shield. The *malu kutjara* drew these on the rocks so that men could see them and so they would learn how to make boomerangs. Boomerangs are now part of *"maluku law"* that is a precedent to be followed laid down in the Dreaming by the mythical ancestral kangaroos. The shape of the engravings is similar to the present general shape of boomerangs. Because the engravings are of plain boomerangs without designs some of the men state that it is *"maluku law"* that they shall make plain boomerangs.

Tindale (1936:184) notes how in the important myth of the *Wati Kutjara* a magical boomerang figures and how the ancestral path of the *wati kutjara* was to the north and west of the Pitjantjatjara area but then passed through the Warburton Ranges where the boomerang was unknown to the people in 1935.

With regard to the origins of the fluted boomerang this would appear to be the result of influence from central Australia as the design is similar to specimens described by Spencer and Gillen (1899:596). The geometric zig zag type pattern on the decorated boomerang is similar to the types of designs found in Western Australia (Strehlow 1964:57).

Conclusions

Just how long the Pitjantjatjara have made or used boomerangs in something resembling the modern form is in my view still an open question. It could be stated that this period has been long enough for the design to be passed down for at least one or two generations and long enough for the boomerang to be incorporated in the people's mythology but this in itself is not an argument for great antiquity.

Plate 6.6:6 More precise shaping with a tomahawk.

Plate 6.6:7 A rasp is used to finish the weapon.

6.7 SHIELD (Tjara)

Description

The Pitjantjatjara make a number of large mulga or blood wood shields. Whilst there are wide variations in size they conform generally to the patterns shown in figure 6.7:1. The distinctive features are the protruding handle type, the face of which may be flat, slightly convex or slightly concave, and the use of both the face and the back to incise a variety of designs. The designs vary from the Western Australian geometric type which cover the whole face, to the central Australian type with symbolic representations of animal tracks, men, camps, etc. which relate to the stories and myths of the people. (Strehlow [1964:57] and Munn [1964:20-30]). Analysis of the symbolism of these graphic representations and their relationship to the Western Desert mythology is beyond the scope of this paper.

In dimension the shields vary from 65 cm to 90 cm in length, 12 cm to 17 cm in breadth and are generally about 1.5cm in thickness. The weight varies from about 1.1 kg to 1.6 kg. The shields are made primarily for sale although I am told they are sometimes still used in ceremonies but have not witnessed this.

Method of Manufacture

This is very similar to the method described for the spear thrower and the boomerang although a larger and thicker flitch of timber is removed from the mulga or blood wood tree (plate 6.7:2). Most of the shaping is done with a toma-hawk (plates 6.7:2-3) with a chisel being used to shape the handle (plate 6.7:4) and a narrow chisel for the incised designs (plate 6.7:5).

Historical Information

As with the boomerang the shield has been recorded by all early observers as absent from the peoples material culture. This is not surprising as it would be an extremely cumbersome and heavy article for the people to carry. Again like the boomerang the old people insist that their fathers made shields and it also figures in the myth of the *malu kutjara*. The shield also figures in the Pitjantjatjara myth "The punishment of Mamuru" (Berndt — 1964:340).

It is essentially a spear shield rather than a parrying shield and compares closely with early museum specimens from Western Australia although these have a more pronounced geometrical fluting and zigzag design (Von Brandenstein 1972:223-238).

Conclusions

Similar remarks to those made for the boomerang are applicable. Its antiquity in the area is open to question but evidence of design would appear to indicate diffusion or trade from the west as the source of its introduction.

However, in the present craft context the shield is an example of patient and skilful craftsmanship with the probability that the designs still retain a great deal of mythological significance.

Plate 6.7:2 A large flitch of Mulga wood being roughly trimmed.

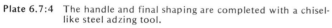

Plate 6.7:4 The handle and final shaping are completed with a chisel-like steel adzing tool.

Plate 6.7:3 Rough shaping is carried out skilfully with a tomahawk.

Plate 6:7:5 A narrow chisel is used to incise totemic designs on the outer surface.

FIGHTING STICKS AND CLUBS

Several types of fighting sticks and clubs are occasionally made by the Pitjantjatjara. With the exception of a reference by Helms (1896:269) to a simple throwing stick there appears to be no confirmation that any of these fighting sticks or clubs were made and used in their present form traditionally. Each type will be only briefly discussed.

6.8   WOMEN'S FIGHTING STICK *(Kuturu)*

As shown in plate 6.8:1 this is very simply a length of mulga or blood wood which has been planed or scraped down to a circular shape and somewhat irregularly grooved. Both ends are pointed. The specimen shown was 1 m in length has a maximum diameter of 5 cm and weighs 1.5 kg. The people insist it was a traditional weapon but if this were so they would not be carried around but made when required and discarded.

Plate 6.8:1

6.9   FIGHTING CLUB *(Tjutinpa)*

This appears to be an introduced craft item and is referred to only by the English term "nulla nulla". The specimen figured was made from mulga 59 cm in length, handle diameter 2.5 cm with the bulbous head 17 cm in length with a maximum diameter of 7 cm. Total weight 700 g. (see plate 6.9:1). Davidson (1936:79) refers to throwing clubs with bulges cut in the solid but noting that they were absent in this general area.

Plate 6.9:1

6.10 FIGHTING CLUB – ADZE *(Irama)*

This is an unusual weapon made only by two of the older men at Amata. It has more of a sword shape than a club, being 10 cm wide and 2 cm thick in the specimen figured (plate 6.10:1). The length is 95 cm and the weight 900 g. To the handle a semi-discoidal stone flake has been affixed using spinifex gum in identical fashion to the spear thrower. The face has been incised with a geometrical Western Australian type design.

Davidson (1936:78) refers to throwing sticks with gum handles and adze blades as being found in Western Australia, central Australia and northern South Australia. However, the specimen he describes does not have the broad sword-like shape of the specimen below. It is possible that his throwing stick/adze was in fact a club/adze from which the present idea developed. It would appear strange to affix an adze to a throwing stick which would result in the adze-stone and gum fixture requiring continual repair of damage.

Plate 6.10:1

6.11 ADZING TOOL (Kantitjara)

It would appear more likely that a simpler adzing tool (plate 6.11:1) was in use by the Pitjantjatjara traditionally. Helms (1896:270) refers to a flint mounted with gum to a shorter stick and Davidson (1936:77-79) refers to an almost identical implement in the eastern part of the general Pitjantjatjara area.

The specimen pictured is 65 cm long with a diameter of 2.5 cm and a total weight of 450 g. The shaft is generally slightly curved and the adzing flake is set in spinifex gum.

These implements are no longer used but have been entirely replaced by an adaptation in steel (plates 6.11:2). This specimen consists of a 2.5 cm carpenters chisel welded into a length of 2.5 cm pipe 46 cm long.

Plate 6.1:9 shows this type of implement in use. It is of interest to note that in 1903 Basedow (1904:26) found an earlier stage of this adaptation in the Musgrave Ranges. In this case a piece of iron no doubt left by an early explorer had been sharpened and affixed to a length of mulga with kangaroo sinew.

Plate 6.11:1

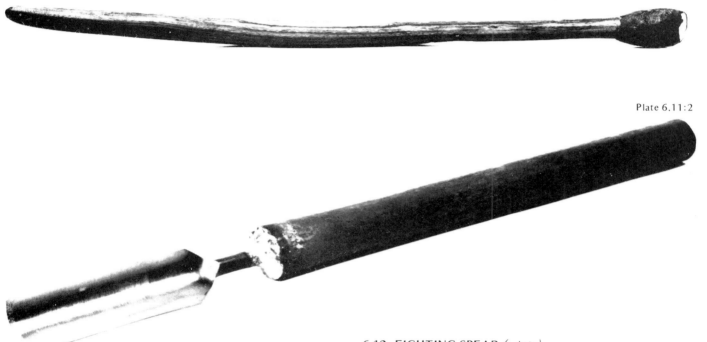

Plate 6.11:2

6.12 FIGHTING SPEAR (winta)

The specimen shown in plate 6.12:1 is made from a single piece of mulga 1.33 m in length, the shaft is 2.5 cm in diameter which is broadened to a flat-pointed head maximum width 4.5 cm and thickness 1 cm. This is brought to a sharp point which is fire hardened. The weapon is made and finished smooth using the adapted chisel adze, rasp or pieces of glass. This specimen was made for sale but this type of spear is still kept and used by the men as a fighting spear. The *wintas* used by the men in spear fights were of similar design but the spear head tended to be narrower (about 3 cm width) so that it could be more readily thrust right through the victims thigh.

It would appear from Davidson (1934:45) that hand spears were traditionally distributed at least in the eastern portion of the Pitjantjatjara area whilst in 1891 Helms (1896:219) reported spears with similar heads from the Blythe Ranges.

Plate 6.12:1

6.13 MANUFACTURE OF SPINIFEX GUM *(kiti)*

It has been noted in the previous sections that an adhesive made from spinifex gum is and was used by the Pitjantjatjara for setting adzing flakes in handles of spear throwers and adzing tools. It is still also used for repairing cracks or plugging knot holes in the wooden bowls *Kanilypa* and *Piti.*

The sources of raw material for the manufacture of *kiti* are globules of gum which exude from the base of the spinifex bush *(Triodia Sp.)* or the granular substance adhering to the small stems of a particular species of bushy desert mulga. Whilst not differentiated botanically from the mulga tree *(Acacia aneura)* used in artifacts manufacture this species is specially identified by the people and called *puyukara.* The eastern Pitjantjatjara favour the use of the spinifex bush as the source of gum whilst the Tomkinson Range Pitjantjatjara appear to use only the mulga bush as a source. According to Greenway (1973:202) the spinifex bush only exudes the globules of gum when particular bushes are attacked by a parasite.

The process of manufacture is said to be essentially the same for each material source and commences with thrashing the mulga bush (plate 6.13:1) or the spinifex needles with a stick onto a piece of canvas or cloth to dislodge the gum. Only the spinifex gum method was witnessed and this is shown in plates 6.13:2-9 . The process is firstly concerned with separating the gum from pieces of vegetable matter and it will be noted that a modern adaptation in the form of a flywire sieve is used. Traditionally this separation would have been performed by winnowing and *kanilypa* separating only. Great skill is required in the heating process by movement of the mulga bark torch across the gum to ensure it is softened sufficiently to be pliable but not over heated which would cause the gum to melt and become brittle and useless on cooling.

Plate 6.13:1 The first stage in one of the methods of manufacture of traditional gum. Thrashing branches of desert mulga to separate particles of gum adhering to the leaves.

Plate 6.13:2 Spinifex bush *triodia busedonii* is another source of traditional adhesive gum.

Plate 6.13:3 Using fly-wire as a sieve.

Plate 6.13:4 Separating the stalks from the gum and chaff.

Plate 6.13:6 Using the *kanilypa* to separate sand and fine debris.

Plate 6.13:5 Crushing the chaff to facilitate sorting.

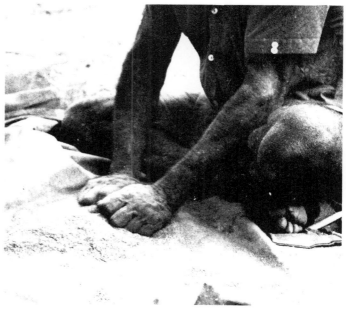

Plate 6.13:7 Burning off the chaff.

Plate 6.13:8 Pounding grain with a hammerstone.

Plate 6.13:9 Forming gum into a compact ball.

Plates 6.13:3-9 Stages in the manufacture of traditional spinifex gum. These photographs show 6.13:3 the initial sieving of stalks of the spinifex bush to which the globules of gum adhere; 6.13:4-5 further crushing and separating the chaff; 6.13:6 using a wooden *kanilypa* with a skilful oscillating movement to separate sand and other fine debris; 6.13:7 carefully passing a flame over the remaining gum/chaff mixture to burn out the chaff; 6.13:8 pounding the gum with a hammerstone; 6.13:9 carefully heating the gum so that it can be compacted into a ball.

Plate 6.13:10 Natural gums are used extensively to mount stone tools onto wooden handles.

6.14 ADAPTED CRAFT – ANIMAL CARVINGS

The Pitjantjatjara women sculpt representations of local fauna from solid blocks of mulga, quondong, or blood wood. These include lizards, native cats, wild dogs and the large perenti. The representations are semi abstract and demonstrate a high degree of artistic skill in balancing economy of form with intricate incised designs (see plate 6.14:1).

The animal sculptures vary in size from 15 cm in length up to striking life size perenti (see plate 6.14:2), 90 cm in length and weighing 3.2 kg.

Plate 6.14:1 A fine example of a wooden animal sculpture. Pitjantjatjara women have developed a high degree of skill in sculpturing and decorating a wide range of desert animals.

Plate 6.14:2 A life-size perenti. A further example of Pitjantjatjara sculptured animals.

7

THE GROWTH AND IMPORTANCE OF THE ARTIFACT INDUSTRY

The Pitjantjatjara people have been involved in some form of organised manufacture of craft for sale since 1948 when spinning and weaving of wool was initiated at Ernabella Mission. Creative craft work particularly spinning and weaving, painting and more recently batik has continued ever since with twenty or thirty women being continuously employed on this work. The development of this successful women's adapted craft industry has been chronicalled by Miss Winifred Hilliard (1968) who has fostered and guided this work for over 20 years.

The Pitjantjatjara people at Amata and Pipalyatjara are now making a wide range of high quality traditional and adapted craft. Sixty to seventy men and women are involved in making artifacts in varying quantities. The total income to craftsmen and women from the sale of these artifacts is between $2,000 and $2,500 per month. This successful enterprise is controlled by the Amata Society with guidance and assistance in marketing and accounting provided by the European crafts officer.

The reasons for the development, complete decline, and current successful re-establishment of this industry are relevant to discussion about future problems of development and maintenance of craft or other enterprises.

The first organised craft was initiated around 1968 but the quality was poor and the sales of craft only about $500 per year. In 1969 a crafts officer Mr. David Abrams was appointed to Amata and was able to initiate a dramatic upsurge both in quality and quantity of work. In 1972 Mr. Abrams left Amata and the craft industry collapsed entirely until 1974 when a new crafts officer, Mr. Ushma Scales, was appointed and has successfully revitalised the enterprise. The fluctuations are shown in the graph of annual on page 69.

The relevant questions are how was it possible to develop a successful artifacts industry and why did it collapse when the craft officer support was withdrawn?

Mr. David Hope who was closely involved in the development of the Crafts Industry as Superintendent at Amata states (Hope 1973):—

"Two important factors were responsible for the upsurge of quality and quantity. The first was that production was confined to artifacts as such — that is to the familiar and the traditional. The second was that the quality demanded was very high. Crafts people, it was found, responded gladly to the high standards expected. At the end of 1971 the best producers worked towards presenting an exhibition in Sydney. In this way Aboriginal people at Amata were able to bring their art to European people in Sydney. This process contributed not only to group pride but reinforced the feeling among the people that they had something of real value to contribute to the Australian culture generally."

The other factor not mentioned by Hope but which was self evident during a visit to Amata at that time has to do with black-white relationships. The craftsmen's group-pride developed and flourished only because the attitude of the Europeans involved in the craft work held towards the Aboriginal craftsmen. This attitude of respect and admiration for the quality of their work was quickly perceived by the Aboriginal people. As Stanner (1974:7) has pointed out settlements were "total institutions" with Aboriginals in them living in virtual complete dependency on authority for virtually everything. So the craft industry provided an opportunity for Europeans who were eager to accept it, of reversing the dependence subservience roles between blacks and whites which was a corollary of settlement life.

Despite this progress, both in material and philosophical terms the industry collapsed as soon as the European crafts officer left. Again Hope (1973) suggests some valid reasons as follows:

"The fact that the Amata artifacts industry collapsed when those responsible for its development left indicates that something was fundamentally wrong. In the first place the crafts people were not able to form themselves into a legally autonomous group which could be subsidised; which could employ staff and which could decide and put its own policies into action. Secondly there was no marketing organisation. Thirdly the industry was structured by Europeans in institutional terms and once institutional management failed, so the venture failed."

After a lapse of over a year the industry has been re-established and is flourishing.

It has been possible for the crafts officer, who like the Europeans previously involved, has a genuine respect and admiration for the Aboriginal people and their craft, to quickly re-establish the quality and quantity of output. It is obvious that the people like making craft and that they obtain a great deal of satisfaction and pride from it. This is particularly true of the people in smaller decentralised settlements. The people at Pipalyatjara, both men and women, given the slightest encouragement worked away happily making artifacts. At Cave Hill, a small decentralised settlement 20 km north of Amata, craft has become a major activity with work of high standard and artistic merit being produced.

The work of the Pitjantjatjara craftsmen and women has artistic merit. Statements about artistic merit are open to challenge because they are based on a culturally subjective judgement but there are other reasons why statements about Aboriginal art are challenge which I will pursue taking the small wooden incised animal made at cave Hill and shown in plate 6.14:1 as an example.

The first challenge could well be an aesthetic one. The reader is enjoined to look again at the picture of the animal in isolation as a piece of art and consider whether the artist has achieved a sense of balance and proportion and whether she has been able to impose a heavy busy design comprised only of parts of circles onto a form with simple lines and produce a pleasing unity.

The second challenge could be a suggestion that the piece has no meaning that it is non-traditional and an item made for money. I would contest this challenge strongly on the grounds that any piece of original and distinctive art must have meaning to the artist to be created in the first place. As Tuckson (1964:60) points out "man generally speaking, when he expresses himself through visual form does so in relation to his environment. Environment involves not only time and place, but also the society in which the artist works as well as his training and knowledge and whatever he absorbs through perception of the outer world". The sculpture of the animal is abstract yet part of the artist's environment, the circle design is abstract yet the circle is very much part of the symbolism of the artist's people. The care and complete absorption in their work that is obvious when watching Pitjantjatjara craftsmen, confirm that these works are conscious and meaningful creations reflecting the artist's personality and total environment. I would further observe that the people are demonstrably very happy, when group cohesion is strong, this is reflected in better and more beautiful works of art and craft.

To suggest that art or craft by Aboriginal people is somehow wrong if it is not traditional as Sandall (1973:1-6) points out, is to give culture an absolute connotation which is good in itself and not an adaptive apparatus serving human needs which can be evaluated on end results.

I am therefore postulating that a well conceived and organised craft industry plays an important role in Pitjantjatjara society in developing both personal and group pride in creative achievement. From this stems dignity, group identity and an opportunity for the people to emerge from a dependent situation.

A craft industry provides also the opportunity to earn money in an occupation that is meaningful and congenial to the people which does not involve a total commitment to the Western industrial type economic activity which involves many participants in working for set hours each day at tasks which may be boring and uncreative.

In making artifacts the craftsman works in an environment of his own choosing.

The autonomy and incorporation of the Pitjantjatjara groups that Hope (1973) mentioned was necessary to avoid future collapses of the industry is now being achieved in principal if not entirely in fact. The craft activities are subsidised by the Government through the Aboriginal Arts Board of the Australia Council and may well need to be for many years to come but in this they are no different to craft associations in European societies. It is the very economics of hand crafts in an industrial automated society that demands assistance from the society for its survival.

The survival of Aboriginal craft industries is essential for as I have shown the preservation of Aboriginal crafts plays a vital role in the preservation of Aboriginal Society itself.

APPROXIMATE VALUE ARTIFACT SALES   AMATA

FIGURE 3

In this final section I will outline the problems remote groups of Pitjantjatjara are facing and discuss some ways in which they may be helped to survive. The decentralisation initiative being taken by the Pitjantjatjara and hundreds of other tribal Aboriginals living on missions and settlements elsewhere in Australia, is the last chance the people will have to survive as separate self-determining peoples. If it fails the destruction of Aboriginal society, which began with inhumanity and conquest but none the less has been pursued consciously or unconsciously in the name of humanity ever since, will be completed.

The most crucial and damning problem is one which Australian Society itself has to solve. This is for the white community to decide that is wants Aboriginal Society to survive. There is sufficient evidence from history and current attitudinal studies to suggest that a large section of the community are yet to be convinced of the merit of this proposition. One of the main reasons for this is that attempts to mould public opinion to support the preservation of Aboriginal Society have been largely based on appeals to public morality. Either we should preserve Aboriginal Society because we owe it to them or more often we should preserve their society so they can in turn enjoy the benefits and joys of our own great society. That this approach is doomed to failure in a society which is based on acquisition of personal wealth and material possessions seems obvious.

A demonstrably valid proposition which is hopefully more likely to be accepted by the community in the long term is that knowledge of and contact with Aboriginal Society, albeit itself changing, can benefit and enrich the total Australian Society. Whilst this is implicit in much that has been written about Aboriginal religion, social structure and art it is seldom explicated. On the other hand a somewhat parallel but narrower proposition that European migration to Australia has bestowed benefits of diversification and enrichment to our society is often propounded and receives some measure of acceptance.

A heavy responsibility rests on the unfortunately small band of people who have some understanding and appreciation of the depth and richness of Aboriginal culture. The responsibility is to do all in their power to communicate this knowledge effectively and widely so that the inaccurate stereotype of Aboriginals and their society as backward and primitive can be methodically destroyed. This responsibility is being accepted by many scholars and teachers but this work needs to be stepped up a hundred fold because with respect to the western Pitjantjatjara, time is not on their side. The rate of externally stimulated change is increasing year by year as more money and more Europeans are descending on Aboriginal communities in the name of progress.

To demonstrate the validity of the proposition that the total Australian society can learn and profit from Aboriginal society I will quote one or two authorities to demonstrate the point.

Maddock (1972:177-194) concludes a lucid discussion of "progress" in terms of social philosophy by stating that Aboriginal society has "exemplary value as a model exhibiting many features of social freedom, the realization of which has usually only been speculated upon in Western thought."

An authority in the field of art,Tuckson (1964:68) concludes an analysis of Aboriginal Art and the Western World in the following words: "We have a rich heritage the greater part of which remains neglected. And even if this is not specifically our own heritage, there is no question at all that it will come to have a much greater bearing on our own Australian art in the years to come."

It is in the field of art that most progress has been made in terms of recognition. The support given by the Australian Government through the Aboriginal Arts Board to Aboriginal artists, musicians, writers, craftsmen and dancers, has not only been responsible for many Aboriginal communities being able to maintain some dignity and pride in their own achievements but through display and exhibitions, is helping greatly towards a European understanding of Aboriginal culture.

I have placed great emphasis on the recognition of the value of Aboriginal society by the community and the development by the community of a desire for Aboriginal society to survive. Without it the efforts of Aboriginal groups themselves will be consciously and unconsciously frustrated by Governments, administrations, missionaries and "do-gooders" as they have so often been in the past.

Despite efforts being undertaken to educate the general community about Aboriginal Society, significant attitudinal changes will take a long time. The only hope for the survival of decentralised communities, or indeed of an identifiable Aboriginal Society rests with Governments, particularly the Australian Government, taking decisive action to respond to the wishes of tribal Aboriginal people before it is too late. Some of the actions which should be undertaken with a sense of urgency are as follows:

■ The Australian Government should take immediate steps to ensure that its stated policy of encouraging and assisting the decentralisation initiative is carried out. If the experiences of the Pitjantjatjara is any guide their desire to return to their own lands has been continually obstructed by disinterest. I have mentioned how the Kunamatta people have been trying for years to obtain some minimal facilities so that they can return and live at Kunamatta. At a Pan-Pitjantjatjara conference held with Government officials at Ernabella in July 28-30 1975, the same desires were again strongly articulated by groups of Pitjantjatjara men from Coffin Hill, Wingellina, Lake Wilson, Katala and Mambanyi. A recurring theme expressed by the Pitjantjatjara at this conference was "How many times do we have to tell you these things before you will believe us?"

■ It is essential that the general public and in particular those involved in Aboriginal affairs have an understanding of tribal Aboriginals and their decentralization initiative. Too often when a decentralized settlement has been established there is a tendency for people to pursue the people with elements of Western Society. There is a danger of such settlements becoming replicas of existing settlements with stores, schools, hospitals and a plethora of Europeans. The much publicised policy of Aboriginal self-determination will then become nothing more than a meaningless charade with the people having little alternative left but to submit to the pressures of modernisation and assimilation.

In a most perceptive article Hamilton (1972:39) summed up this process as follows:
"The policy of assimilation . . . seeks to bring about not a new type of social system but the total disappearance of the minority group and the complete eradication of its social and cultural existence. Even if such a procedure is defensible, the evidence is that the means tried in the past, and those relied on today — welfare, health and education services in particular, do not bring about the desired end; they simply result in social chaos".

Tragically Hamilton's predictions are being borne out as some decentralised settlements initiated by Aboriginal people with such high hopes are showing signs of disintegration and social chaos under the pressure of externally introduced change.

■ Most importantly the Australian Government, the State Governments and through them the hopefully fewer Europeans who come in contact with tribal Aboriginal groups, must realise that to insist on pressuring Aboriginal groups to alter their own society to conform to the values and practices of our society is to destroy Aboriginal Society just as effectively and even more rapidly than our ancestors did for most Aboriginal groups with guns, disease and appropriation of lands. Again as Hamilton (1972:39) succinctly points out "Social change which stems from the needs and desires of the people themselves is a different matter. Where people wish to alter their circumstances both as individuals and groups they are likely to find ways of effectively mediating the conflicts bought about by contact between two alien systems, without such mediation being destructive. Such change is usually rapid in some spheres, such as the material, and slow in others, such as belief systems. Nonetheless it is the only form of change which has the potential for continuity without destruction".

In summary the Pitjantjatjara are asking very little. They want support to enable them to form their own communities in their own lands and they want tolerance and understanding from the Europeans who are sent out to give them the support they require. Given these things and provided they are also given inviolate security of ownership of their lands the Pitjantjatjara (and the tribal groups still remaining elsewhere) have every chance of survival.

The Pitjantjatjara have many strengths which will help them in this struggle. Their social and ritual structures are still largely intact, as is the relationship between the men and their land which provides the core for their whole religious belief system. The desire of small groups not only to return to their own country but also to succeed in setting up their own decentralised communities remains strong and unswerving.

This is not to suggest that the Aboriginal people are unaware of the many problems they will have to solve in their new situation. There will be problems of leadership and authority particularly in relation to the control of community property such as vehicles.

There will be problems imposed by the environment particularly if severe droughts occur which will diminish the availability of bush foods. However, this problem may be alleviated by assisting the people to develop irrigated gardens. A successful garden has been in operation at Ernabella for some years and some of the men who want to return to Kunamatta have asked for help to do likewise. Whilst these would be small and employ few people they would provide an essential ingredient for an improvement in diet and health.

There will be great problems in meeting the educational and vocational aspirations of the young without alienation from the community. This hopefully will only be a short term problem as Aboriginals with the necessary skills replace Europeans, and as in the longer term the communities themselves change and develop from within. The present high rate of population growth and consequent "younging" of the Aboriginal population will aggravate this problem.

My firm view is that the Pitjantjatjara people will be able to solve these problems and self-determining communities like Pipalyatjara will survive. But this can only happen if the European administrators provide the sort of climate to let it happen. The necessary climate is one of tolerance, patience and understanding that the solutions the people themselves develop may be quite different to Western orientated solutions which should not be forced on the people.

I am led to this view because of the observable and expressed determinations of the people themselves to survive and succeed as self determining Aboriginal groups in their own traditional land. Because it would appear that the Pitjantjatjara peoples conduct is still largely governed by adherence to the order of things laid down for all time by the Ancestors it is possible that solutions to these new problems will be found by remodelling existing laws and norms to fit these new situations. Such a solution would maintain the unity between religious and secular conduct and avoid the collapse of their religion which in other areas has preceded the break up of the groups society.

Whatever solutions the people choose it is important that they be given time to develop and test them without excessive external pressure. By this I am not advocating the people be left to sink or swim on their own which is the catchcry of the many European cynics and the "I told you so" brigade when failures occur. Rather the remote groups need an unobtrusive and sympathetic European presence at this stage to provide the accounting , administrative and mechanical skills which in many areas we have studiously avoided imparting to the people during their long institutionalisation.

REFERENCES

Basedow H.: 1904. "Anthropological notes made on the South Australian Government north-west prospecting expedition." *Transaction of the Royal Society of South Australia.* Vol. 28 (pp 12-51).

Bates Daisy M.: 1921. "Ooldea water". *Royal Geographical Society of Australasia, South Australian Branch Proceedings.* Vol. 21 (pp 73-78).

Berndt R.M.: 1941. "Tribal migrations and myths centering on Ooldea, South Australia". *Oceania.* Vol. 12 (1) (pp 1-20).

Berndt R.M.: 1959. "The concept of the tribe in the western desert of Australia". *Oceania.* Vol. 30 (2) (pp 81-107).

Berndt R.M. and C.H.: 1964. *The world of the first Australians.* Ure Smith, Sydney.

Berndt R.M.: 1965. "Law and order in Aboriginal Australia". *Aboriginal man in Australia.* Eds. R.M. and C.H. Berndt. Angus and Robertson.

Biskup P.: 1973. *Not slaves not citizens.* University of Queensland Press.

Carruthers J.: 1892. Report. *South Australian Parliamentary Papers* (179).

Cleland J.B.: 1966. "The ecology of the Aboriginal in South and Central Australia". *Aboriginal man in South and Central Australia.* Ed. B.C. Cotton, Government Printer, Adelaide. (pp 111-157).

Coombs H.C.: 1973. "Decentralisation trends amongst Aboriginal communities" *Aboriginal News.* Vol. 1 (3).

Davidson D.S.: 1934. "Australian spear traits and their derivations". *Polynesian Society Journal* Vol. 43 (pp 41-72; pp 143-162).

Davidson D.S.: 1936. "The spear thrower in Australia". *Proceedings of the American Philosophical Society.* Vol. 76 (4) (pp 445-483).

Davidson D.S.: 1936. "Australian throwing sticks — throwing clubs and boomerangs". *American Anthropologist.* Vol. 38 (1) (pp 76-100).

Douglas W.H.: 1964. "An introduction to the western desert language". *Oceania Linguistics Monograph.* No. 4.

Duguid C.: 1972. *The Doctor and the Aborigines.* Rigby Ltd., Adelaide.

Elkin A.P.: 1939. "Kinship in South Australia". *Oceania.* Vol. 10 (2) (pp 196-234).

Elkin A.P.: 1964. *The Australian Aborigines.* Fourth Edition, Angus and Robertson, Sydney.

Finlayson H.H.: 1935. *The Red Centre.* Angus and Robertson, Sydney.

Foley J.C.: 1957. "Droughts in Australia." *Bureau of Meteorology Bulletin* No. 43.

Gould R.A.: 1967. "Notes on hunting, butchering and sharing of game among the Ngatatjara and their neighbours in the West Australian desert". *Kroeber Anthropological Society Papers.* Vol. 36 (pp 41-66).

Gould R.A.: 1968. "Preliminary report on excavations at Puntutjarpa rock-shelter, near the Warburton Ranges, W.A." *Archeology and Physical Anthropology in Oceania* Vol. 3 (3) (pp 161-185).

Gould R.A.: 1969. *Yiwara: Foragers of the Australian desert.* Collins, London.

Gould R.A.: 1969. "Subsistence behaviour among the western desert Aborigines of Australia". *Oceania.* Vol. 39 (4) (pp 253-274).

Gill Walter: 1970. *Peterman journey,* Rigby Ltd., Adelaide.

Graydon W.L.: 1956. *Report of the select committee appointed to inquire into the native welfare conditions in the Laverton-Warburton Range area.* Government Printer, Perth.

Graydon W.L.: 1957. *Adam and atoms.* Daniels, Perth.

Greenway J.: 1973. *Down among the wildmen.* Hutchinson of Australia.

Hamilton Annette: 1972. "Blacks and whites: the relationships of change" *Arena* No. 30.

Hamilton Annette: 1971. *Socio-cultural factors in health among the Pitjantjatjara.* Mimeo (pp 1-18).

Helms R.: 1896. "Anthropology report of Elder scientific expedition 1891". *Royal Society of South Australia, Transactions.* Vol. 16 (3) (pp 237-332).

Hiatt L.R.: 1962. "Local organisation among the Australian Aborigines". *Oceania.* Vol 32 (4) (pp 267-286).

Hilliard W.: 1968. *The people in between.* Hodder and Stoughton, London.

Hope D.A.C.: 1973. "Amata artifacts industry". Report to national seminar Aboriginal Arts in Australia, Aboriginal Arts Board, Canberra.

Johnston T.H.: 1941. "Some aboriginal routes in the western portion of South Australia". Proceedings of the *Royal Geographical Society of Australia, South Australian Branch,* Vol. 42 (pp 33-65).

Kirke D.K.: 1974. "The traditionally orientated community" Pt. 2.1. *Better health for aborigines.* Ed. Hetzel, B.S. et al. University of Queensland Press.

Lee R.B. and De Vore I.: 1968. Discussions Pt. II 9c. "Does hunting bring happiness". *Man the hunter* (pp 89-95) Aldine Press.

Long J.P.M.: 1963. "Preliminary work in planning welfare development in the Peterman Ranges" *Australian Territories.* Vol. 3 (2) (pp 4-12).

Love J.R.B.: 1942. "A primitive method of making a wooden dish by native women of the Musgrave Ranges, South Australia." *Transactions Royal Society of South Australia.* Vol. 66 (pp 215-217).

Maddock Kenneth.: 1972. *The Australian Aborigines: a portrait of their society.* Allen Lane, Penguin Press, London.

Mabbutt J.A.: 1971. "The arid zone as a prehistoric environment". *Aboriginal man and environment in Australia.* Mulvaney D.J. and J. Golson, Eds.

McCarthy F.D.: 1940. "Aboriginal material culture: causative factors in its composition." *Mankind.* Vol. 2 (8) (pp 241-269), Vol. 2 (9) (pp 294-320).

McCarthy F.D. and Margaret McArthur: 1960. "The food quest and the time factor in Aboriginal economic life". *Records of the American-Australian expedition to Arnhem Land* Vol. 2, Anthropology and Nutrition, Melbourne University Press.

McCarthy F.D.: 1961. "The Boomerang". *Australian Museum Magazine* Vol. 13, (11) (pp 343-349).